Suzanne

Carrie and Glenda
it was great to meet you
and to find you have a
Mennonite background. You will
see a few notes I've added recently,
to give a little background on
Ukraine and Russia.
Regards Gary-

Suzanne

A Remarkable Life

(1909 – 1978)

Gary Vliet - 2014

Suzanne - A Remarkable Life (1909 – 1978)

Copyright 2014 by Gary Vliet

ISBN – 13: 978-1-4921-4883-8

This first edition is published through CreateSpace.Com

Front cover: picture from the "Trek" in late fall 1943, obtained from Conrad Grebel University College. Suzanne is the woman in the black coat walking beside the cow and her sister-in-law Maria is driving the wagon. Not evident in the photo is that there were no able-bodied men on the Trek, as they had been taken to Siberia several years earlier.

Back cover: Map of Suzanne's travels drawn by the author.

Cover background .... sunflowers near Konteniusfeld.

For Arthur, Evelyn, Patti and Jim, and Arthur and Evelyn's
grandchildren Alex, Nadia, Andrew and Connor,
who are kin to Suzanne

for

Les, Donna, Kirsten, Joanne and David,
who were fortunate to have known Suzanne

for

Anna, Abbey, Katelyn and Andrew,
who may get to know their Great-Grandmother through her story

and for

the Nicholson clan,
who have many fond memories of Suzanne.

Contents

FOREWORD

Suzanne Penner was born March 18, 1909 in the Village of Konteniusfeld near Tokmak, which is in the southern region of Ukraine near the Black Sea. Konteniusfeld was one of about 65 Mennonite villages of the Molotschna settlement, which was established in the 1800's.

Suzanne experienced the revolution, the civil war and the collectivization of her village. After her village was collectivized in 1930, Suzanne spent almost three years (Jan 1931 - mid 1933) in Makeyevka working for a German company, which was building a coke factory. From there she went to Kropotkin in the Caucasus to work for a few months with a German woman who was developing better soya and other plants for Russia. She returned to Konteniusfeld in the autumn of 1933 and worked on the collective for about a year.

An opportunity in Leningrad became available in 1934 and she traveled there to work for an English woman, "Lady Muriel". There she met Gena Stelzig and they were married in 1935. Their son Arthur was born June 20, 1939. On June 19, 1941 Suzanne and Arthur left for the Ukraine for a summer visit with Suzanne's family, as Suzanne had not been home for seven years and her family had not yet seen Arthur or met Gena. Gena was to accompany her, but at the last minute he could not, due to a commitment where he worked. On arriving in Konteniusfeld on June 22, 1941, Suzanne discovered that Germany had declared war on the Soviet Union during her trip, and thereafter, travel was frozen and communication was minimal. Other than a couple of telegrams from Gena, she did not see or hear from him again.

Suzanne spent a bit over two years in Konteniusfeld. Four months after arriving, the area was overrun by the German army in October 1941. When the Germans were unable to take

vii

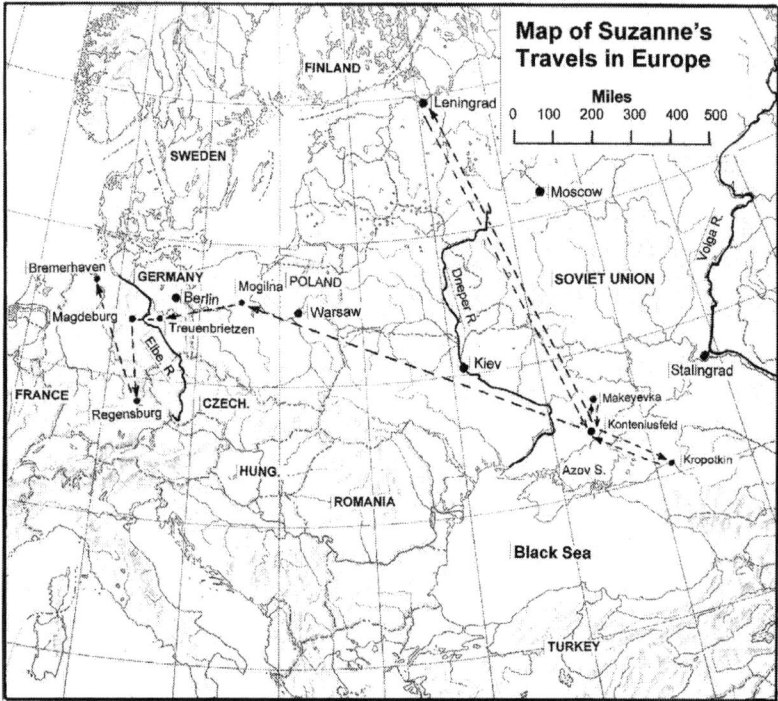

Map of Suzanne's travels in Russia, as well as her "Trek" into Poland, and then into 'East' Germany and finally West Germany.

Stalingrad and were forced to retreat, Suzanne and the rest of the Mennonite community were forced by the Germans to retreat with them. This is known as the "Trek" which started in October 1943 and ended near the Polish border just before Christmas in 1943. After a few months, in March 1944 she and Arthur were forced to move by train into Poland to Mogilno. They were there for about 8 months until January 1945, when they were forced again to flee into what would be East Germany. After a few months near Berlin, in May 1945 they were overrun by the Russians as the war ended and she found herself in the 'Eastern Zone'.

After spending about six months under Russian occupation and fearing they would discover she was from the Ukraine and force her to return, she and Arthur were able to make their escape to West Germany in February 1946. They settled near Regensburg with some relatives and friends until October 1948, when they were able to immigrate to Canada, where they settled in Pincher Creek, Alberta.

In 1957 Suzanne married Clark Vliet and they, with her son Arthur and Clark's son Leslie, moved to Berkeley, California. After graduating from the University of California, Berkeley in 1962, Arthur took a job with DuPont in Brockville, Ontario. Arthur married Evelyn Leggett in 1965 and they have two children. Thus, Suzanne was able, through her determination, to achieve her primary desire, a good life for her son! Suzanne passed away in Oakland, California June 2, 1978 and is buried in Oakland's Mountain View Cemetery.

While each member of the Mennonite community, which made the 'trek' out of the Ukraine, has a unique story, I feel Suzanne's is particularly unusual. Most of those on the trek had spent essentially their entire lives in the Molotschna settlement and had little experience beyond that community, while Suzanne had spent a couple years working in Makeyevka, several months working in the Caucasus and then almost seven years in Leningrad, before returning to Konteniusfeld in 1941. A primary reason she and Arthur became part of the trek was that, rather than waiting until her husband Gena could accompany them, she and Arthur left to visit her family in the Ukraine just two days before Germany's surprise invasion of the Soviet Union. It is amazing what a difference a few days can make to one's life! If she'd waited for Gena to accompany them, would she have been trapped in the Leningrad siege or shipped back east of the Urals ... and would Gena have accompanied her ... probably not, based on Soviet policy? And in the fall of 1941, if the train at Stulnjevo had not been sabotaged just minutes before it was to leave with thousands of Mennonites, she and Arthur would likely have been shipped back east of the Urals. And in the subsequent four years before emigrating to Canada, there were several instances where a difference of a few days or hours, a chance comment by a friend or just being fortunate in some other way made the difference between success and failure. But through it all it was Suzanne's intelligence, resourcefulness, determination and faith that made it possible for her to eventually succeed in her quest.

Suzanne had an eventful life and was loved by those of us who were fortunate to have known her. She is an unforgettable person!

Suzanne ... taken most likely in Makeyevka in 1932 when she was about 23. This is the earliest picture of her that has survived. Amazingly, this photo weathered the 14 turbulent years it took her to finally escape to West Germany in 1946.

Suzanne

1. Childhood

I was born on March 18, 1909 in the village of Konteniusfeld*, near the city of Tokmak in southern Ukraine not far from the Sea of Azov. There were 65 Mennonite** villages in this area and these villages were very nicely arranged. Further from our village there were some Russian villages and towns. Our people were very good farmers, and my parents and grandparents had worked very hard. My grandparents had cut their grain with a sickle and did the threshing by rolling a big rolling stone over the wheat by hand. When I was growing up we had reaping machines and threshing machines, and some people had binders, and some even had tractors. The soil in the Ukraine

----

* Konteniusfeld (Zaporizhia Oblast, Ukraine) was a Mennonite village of the Molotschna settlement in south Ukraine. It was founded in 1821 and named after Samuel Kontenius. The western boundary of this major Mennonite settlement was the Molotschna River. Konteniusfeld is located 10 miles (16 km) from Stulnjevo, where there is a railway station. The village's population before World War I was 507. It comprised 6,356 acres (another source says 8618 acres) of land before the Revolution. The village had a church and an elementary school. The principal industries were the culture of wheat, cattle, fruit, and bees, and at one time there was a large shop, which manufactured farm machinery. (From the Global Anabaptist Mennonite Encyclopedia, Ref. 8) Abram Kasper's brick factory was also a significant industry. A map of the Molotschna settlement is shown on next page.

** See Chapter 18 for a brief history of Mennonites in Russia.

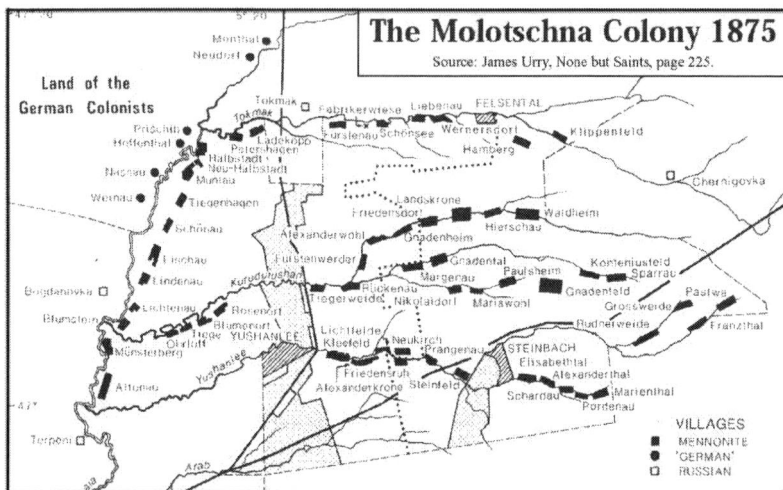

The Molotschna Colony 1875

Source: James Urry, None but Saints, page 225.

The Molotschna Colony as of 1875. Konteniusfeld and Sparrau are located near the middle-right. The part-year stream adjacent to them is the Kutudujuschan, and the larger stream it empties into on the left is the Molotschna River, for which the colony was named. Along the west side of the Molotschna there were several German-Lutheran communities. There were also a few Russian villages on the periphery. From Refs. 5 & 6. Used with permission.

was black and rich. Our area was called the "Breadbasket of Russia". We did not have irrigation, so our crops depended on the rain. Our people built their villages and they were very beautiful. Every house had a fruit yard and also a big vegetable garden. In the springtime when these fruit trees and flowers in the garden were in bloom, it looked so good and the air so clean and that aroma from the flowers was heavenly and the birds were singing!

No wonder that it was called the flowering garden of the Ukraine. We did not have any wild timber near us. We planted our own timber and had several acres of it. The boys and girls all worked on the farm and had to do all the chores and were quite happy. In every village there was a church and also a school.

2

Some of the bigger villages had high schools and colleges. Our village had a church and a school. Just 4 kilometers from our village in Gnadenfeld there was a Mennonite college. The nearest railroad station to us was in Stulnjevo about 18 kilometers away. About 75 kilometers to the northwest in Halbstadt there was a university. Berdjansk was another city about 75 kilometers to the southeast of us on the Azov Sea, and Stutmark was about 40 kilometers away. We would transfer our grain by horses to Berdjansk where we sold it. In the summers, sometimes we would swim in the Azov Sea, which was beautiful. There was no river near Konteniusfeld, only a little creek (called Kutudujuschan), which dried out in the summer. We couldn't swim in the creek, because it was too low and muddy. In the winter the young people did some skating on it.

The house that I was born in was made of mud bricks with plaster on the outside, and was painted each year with whitewash. I loved that house! We had lots of trees around the house. The house had six rooms, but not very big and only four rooms were heated. There was a barn attached to the house. We sold this house and land in 1925 to Henry Dick and bought a larger house from Abe Kasper about 1/2 kilometer to the west. We were about in the middle of the village and across from the school. The new house cost 4500 rubles. We did not (or were not able to) pay off all of this, as it was taken away from us in 1930. There were 32 hectares of land with the house. There was a second small brick house (three rooms and a kitchen) next door to our house which Isaac and his wife Marie occupied. Isaac had 16 hectares of land a little way away. Peter and his wife, Suzanne, bought a little house on the west end of the village with 16 hectares.

Our later house included a barn where we kept the cows and horses (following page). A hall connected the house and barn and there was also an iron door to prevent fire from spreading between the barn and house. Our barn looked good and clean, as also did our pig house. We had about 12 horses, 3

3

or 4 cows, and 4 or 5 pigs, which were for our own use. There were separate buildings for the pigs and chickens and they were also made of brick. We didn't raise these animals for sale, but did sell them when it was necessary. We also had geese, and ducks, but also mostly for our own use. We just had enough animals for our own meat, milk, butter and eggs. Sometimes we would sell eggs and butter when buyers came to the village and transported them by wagon to the Russian cities. Henry Dick would come around each Saturday to buy butter and eggs and sometimes we would sell to him if we had extra.

There were six rooms in our house, all big rooms. We also had a very big summer kitchen where we would bake and cook in the summer. One of the rooms was a kind of dining room, very big, where we all ate in the summer. But in the winter when it was cold, we ate in rooms that also served as living rooms. There were bedrooms for the parents, for grandmother, for the girls and for the boys. One room was a living room, but was used mostly by grandmother. There was an extra room, used as a bedroom, living room or for whatever was needed. Our situation was different than in America. We slept three and four in one room, two in each bed, and some rooms served for sleeping, dining and living. Beds were like benches with a top that lifted up and a lower part that pulled out. We had outside toilets.

In our family* there were 9 children, my grandmother (Gertrude Koop Penner, father's mother) and my parents (Peter and Marie (Franzen)), so there were 12 people living in the same house. The children, in order, were: Isaac, Peter, Elizabeth, Gertrude, Maria, Katherine, Abraham, me (Suzanne), and Sara. My parents' first child died early. We slept four in a room and 2 in each bed. Some of my brothers and sisters got married, so there were not always twelve people at home.

----

* See Chapter 17 for more information on Suzanne's family.

Machines and Feed

North ?

One of these Grandmas the other an extra

Sun Porch

Boys Room

Welkcows

Harness

B.R.

B.R.

Oven

Horses

Dining Room (for eating in summer)

B.R. L.R. Eating

B.R. L.R. Eating

To Root Cellar

Summer Kitchen

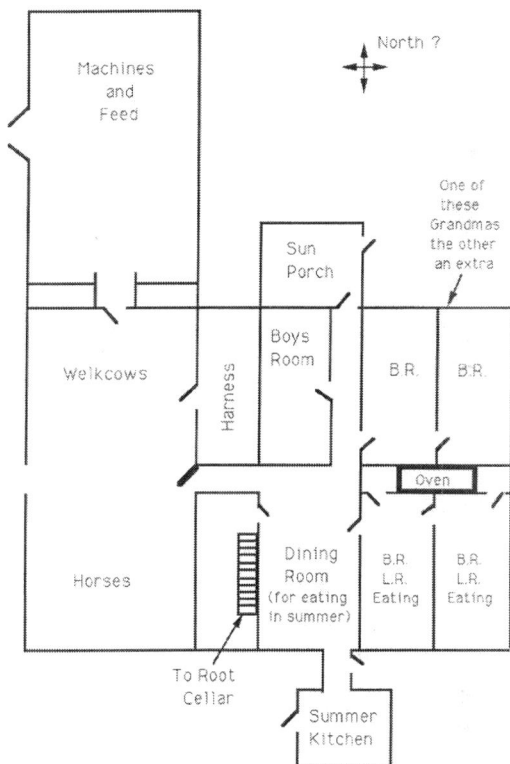

The last (senior) Penner House in Konteniusfeld according to Suzanne. Peter Penner (Suzanne's nephew) indicated the house to be more "linear" than shown here, and I suspect he is correct, as Suzanne referred to a hall and iron door separating the stables. But this is as Suzanne described it. There were also other separate brick buildings for the pigs and chickens.

As a little girl I was, well, half boyish ... I acted more like a boy than a girl. There wasn't a tree around the house that Suzanne hadn't climbed. I also enjoyed playing soldier. I liked to play ball and soldiers with the boys and I made my own toy gun out of wood ... it was not very much to look at. My sister

Gertrude laughed when she saw us small girls marching and playing war. In the spring we all, boys and girls, worked in the fields. I often got to ride a horse or sit on the plow or a seeding machine or drive the horse. We rode horses a lot.

Some villages were very strict and some were not. Our village wasn't. I did not dance, but my sister Sara did. My father was a very good dancer, so I heard, but I hadn't seen him dance.

We had school on the weekdays and also half day on Saturday. On Monday the first class was Bible study. At school we learned both the German and the Russian languages and we had men for teachers. Our teachers were mean! One time we had a young woman teacher, a Russian, who taught the Russian language. She was very pretty and nice, but was strict and hot tempered.

The winter was 3 to 4 months long, and sometimes we had lots of snow and bad winds too, but usually the winters were not too hard. We had lots of fun with sleds and sleigh rides and things like that. And sometimes in the spring when it was very muddy and the wheels of the wagon would get stuck, kids would ride to school on horses and that was fun too. In the winter the girls learned to sew, knit, crochet, embroidery and spin wool.

And Christmas, oh Christmas was nice. We always had three days at Christmas for holidays. The school had a big program on Christmas Eve (the 24th) and a large "community" Christmas tree, which the village bought, because not everyone could afford one. A few families had "wacholder" bushes for Christmas trees in their houses, but we did not. We didn't have Christmas trees around us, so the village had to send someone to get the tree from Felsenthal*. I don't know how far away it was, but it was quite far. Money would be gathered from the families

---

* Felsenthal means "the place of granite", and lies on the northern edge in the Molotschna colony. It was a private estate known for its fruit trees.

in the village, whoever could afford it, and from the mayor, to pay for the tree, cookies, candy, nuts and apples. As a gift we would maybe get a storybook or a picture, which were religious, or maybe a game, apples, nuts or candy. The program would have the Christmas story and poems and carols presented by the children.

In addition to the school program, we had a Christmas program for the youth in the evening on Christmas day in the Mennonite Bretheren Church, which was between Konteniusfeld and Sparrau and used by both villages. Isaac, Henry Penner (the teacher) and some others organized the young people to put on a religious program. There were no gifts. At church we also had a tree and the tree stayed up from Dec 24 until Three Kings Day, about a week after New Years.

At home we prepared very much for Christmas, and had everything baked and done before Christmas day. We cooked either a big ham, ducks or geese and also prepared smoked sausage, sweet-sour cabbage with sugar beets, potatoes and gravy, black (rye) bread, white (wheat) bread, cookies, candy and "fruit soup". Fruit soup had 6 or 7 kinds of dried fruit ... apples, pears, apricots, sour cherries, prunes, raisins and currents, which were simmered in water, and then sugar and cornstarch were added. On the day before Christmas at noon we had dinner, and then at 3 or 4 in the afternoon cookies and buns and ersatz coffee or milk. Ersatz coffee was not real coffee as we have here, since it was made from grain. Then we would get all bathed and washed, and at 5 o'clock we went to school to get our Christmas presents and present our program. It was really fun!

On Christmas day we got up and made the fires, fed the chickens, horses, pigs and cows and then came in and got washed up. The night before Christmas our parents would put plates on the table in the living room and that night Santa would put some small gifts in them. When we could not buy gifts, mother and the older sisters would sew a dress, or knit some socks, hat or cap or mittens and we were happy to get that. The older brothers once made a sled for us. We would open our presents before breakfast. Our presents were like a knitted cap, mittens, scarf or sweater, a dress or a doll, usually made secretly by the older sisters and mother, and mostly what we could use. The gifts would be put on each person's plate on the living room table. We didn't get very much, maybe one or two things. Actually, when Isaac and Peter were younger they had it better, because it was before the Communists.

There were only Mennonites in our villages (those like Konteniusfeld and Sparrau) and the Mennonites kept pretty much to themselves. About in 1924 or 25 a Russian village started between our villages and Waldheim (about 10 km away), but we still didn't associate with them. Maybe the older people were afraid that some girl would marry a Russian - a very sinful thing to do! One Mennonite, Johan Foth, married a Russian girl who was a very good worker and housekeeper, and they lived in our village, but the neighbors would not have very much to do with her. Maybe he couldn't find a Mennonite girl as good as her. This bothered me when I was little. On Sunday we would go to church and be "good" Christians, but wouldn't be nice to this lady or to the Russian workers. This Russian village had good farmers and good farms. Some of the Mennonite farmers hired Russian workers for the harvest time and some stayed to work during the winter too. There never was any real trouble between the Mennonites and the Russians living in the Russian communities. We lived quite peacefully, but separately. There were also poor Russian people that would come from the city and knock on our door and beg for food and other things. We always baked enough that we could feed some of these beggars too.

2. Gathering Clouds

The first big change came with the revolution, which began in 1917. I was 8 years old then. Before that every family would have the Tsar's picture in the living room ... beautiful pictures of the whole family ... the Tsar and Tsarina. I remember when grandmother took them down and burned them and she cried, and I could not understand that. She cried, but she said that we had to do that because there was not a Tsar or a Tsarina any more. And I still can see the pictures on the wall, how beautiful they looked to us.

And then the bandit groups started. One leader was a Russian (a Ukrainian) named Makhno*. He had lived quite far away and had worked for some Mennonites ... took care of their pigs. Maybe they had not treated him right, we don't know exactly. Lots of Mennonites had workers, and I must say honestly and truthfully, some didn't treat the Russian workers right, and they suffered for that later. This Makhno started his bandit groups and they knew exactly where to come in the village. A Russian girl Marusa (Maria) was part of the group, and when men in the village saw her they trembled with fear, she was so brutal. Makhno had a troika (three black horses) that would come in the evenings after sundown, and when the troika appeared you knew there would be shooting and killing. They knew exactly which farmer to go to, because their workers had told them how they had been treated. They murdered some farmers, and stole money, furs and whatever they liked. They would come into a home with their horses and wreck the place,

----

*   Makhno was a Ukrainian anarchist-communist during the Civil War, who fought against all factions attempting to impose authority from outside on the southern Ukraine, even against the Bolsheviks before he finally escaped to Romania in 1921. He was a colorful person and a significant figure during the revolution. (From Wikipedia.)

knock down mirrors and china and take any valuables. The farmers would hide in the timber or in their big gardens or fields. The girls also had to hide, sometimes sleeping all night in the timber. Some families went to the poorer farmers and stayed there over night and came back in the morning to their homes and did their work, and when the evening came they dispersed again. The bandits knew which farmers had treated them badly, and never did come to our house.

My father had helpers mainly in the summer time, two men and a girl who were Russians. I still remember their names: Harmas, a tall blond fellow about 35, an older man about 50 who would always cross himself before he ate, and Helen, also about 35, who was so good to us and was such a help to my mother. Helen stayed over the winter one time. The old man always would say, "Mister Penner (they called us mister) take us again next year". My father always would pay them more than they had agreed to. But I tell you, some people were mean, didn't give them enough to eat, worked them hard and just didn't treat them like human beings. That's why I've often thought it was no wonder that this came up, the bandits and the killing, because they had been treated so badly. And here was one who became the leader of a bandit group. These bandits were not necessarily Communists ... they were just taking advantage of the revolution, and did some bad things. One time they took away some boys that never returned. But they never came to us.

Then the civil war came to our area, the Whites against the Reds (Communists), and it was right in our villages and fields. Our village was full with soldiers, and the fighting went back and forth. In our village one day we had 3 times the Reds and 3 times the Whites. Bullets went through some roofs and the shells from canons exploded in gardens and fields and sometimes in houses too.

One time we had 80 soldiers with their horses around our house and garden. These were the cavalry, and sometimes they stayed for a week or two, all depending on how the battles went.

10

When they came back, some did not come and some were wounded and they had lost some of their horses. The soldiers would take horses from the farmers. We lost most of ours too. Finally, we had just two brood mares and each had a little colt. Elizabeth was afraid that the soldiers would take these two, so she put the two horses in our bedroom during the daytime. The little colts stayed in the barn and at noon we would take the colts to their mothers to get their mother's milk. In the evening we took these colts back to the barn. We put cotton in the horse's ears, so they would not answer a call from the soldiers horses outside. One day one of the horses answered a call from a soldier's horse, and that officer opened the shutters on the windows and looked in the room. Here were Sara and me sitting on the horses and trying to keep them quiet ... feeding them some watermelon and cantaloupe. The officer came in and asked why we had them in the bedroom. Elizabeth explained that she was afraid that some soldier would come and take these horses away from their little colts. The officer was very good and said take the horses back to the barn and if a soldier would try to take them, to tell them they were his. So long as that officer stayed at our place we kept those horses. But later he left and we lost these last two grown horses. Most of our grain was gone too, because the soldiers fed their horses with it.

The soldiers also brought some bad sicknesses, pox and typhus and also some sickness to the cattle, so the farmers lost some of their cows too. In every home there were cases of pox or typhus. In many homes 3 to 5 people got sick, and many families lost 2 or 3 loved ones. There were 4 people in our family sick with typhus: Peter, Katherine, Abraham and Sara. Peter and Katherine were very sick, and we did not expect them to come through, but they did. We did not lose one family member.

After the civil war the Communists took over. In 1921, 22 and 23 we had awfully hard times, because our grain was taken away by the Bolsheviks to feed the people in the cities. Before this, the farmers would sell the wheat, which they didn't need, but

11

would keep enough to eat for one year, in case of bad crops. We did not irrigate and had to depend on rain, but some years it was a dry summer and the crops were bad. So we always kept one year's supply of grain for the family. But the Bolsheviks took everything away and then we had starvation. Thank God we got some help from America, Holland and Germany. Mennonite communities in America sent food parcels to Russia and commune kitchens were opened in each village in the Mennonite communities, but not in the Russian villages. Some of us who had relatives in America got parcels directly. My father had a cousin, Friesen, somewhere in the United States, maybe in Reedley, California, who sent us parcels of food. The parcels had tin milk, which we had never seen before, rice and cocoa and things like that. One time we were told a parcel of clothes was coming and Dad had to go to Halbstadt (about 50 km away) to get it, but the box was empty ... all had been stolen ... a big disappointment to us. These parcels really didn't come very often and there really wasn't much for 12 people, but we were still grateful for it. We maybe got 6 or 7 parcels during one fall and winter. I can still see the big pot of rice mother cooked for our 12 people. She would divide it up, a soup plate full for each, and we put a little sugar and cinnamon on top and it was oh so good! We did not eat it all, we left some for the next day. Because we got these parcels, we could not get anything at the government kitchen, which was for everyone else. Only those who had nothing else to eat could go to the kitchen. You could see these people standing there waiting for a cup of cocoa and a dish of rice. And that saved them.

I have seen such hungry people going around to the houses and begging. Russian mothers from the cities would come to the villages and beg for food ... in the cities you could find practically nothing. These mothers would come with their babies and would pinch them to make them cry, so we would feel sorry for them. And we would give them a slice of bread or an egg ... or might give them something else we had. Sometimes we just had to close the windows or else they would look in when we ate and then we didn't feel very good about it ... we ourselves eating (even though it was only a little) and they were suffering outside and begging for a piece of bread.

Later on, in the winter, we were very hungry ourselves. We each had one little piece of rye bread in the morning, along with some "ersatz" coffee. We would make ersatz coffee by browning wheat or rye and boiling it in water. That was all that we had. And we would go into the fields and look for some green stuff to cook and to eat, like horseradish. You know, people died because of hunger and of eating some of the green stuff, it was terrible. No people in our family died of this. We had the two little colts left from when our horses were taken away during the war, and my brother Isaac often said to Dad, "If we don't get any help, then we will have to kill one of these young horses for food". Lots of people killed their horses for food. If we had not needed the horses for the spring work, we would have done it, because we were very hungry, as we had very little to eat. I remember how my sister Katherine and I found an old beet in the cellar that was practically rotten. We put it in a coal fire and we thought it was delicious! Hard to believe, but it was true. We couldn't go to school anymore, our minds were just not there. The whole talk was just about food and what we had eaten before. There was no other talk.

Then the spring came and the fruit gardens were in bloom. You would see the children and the people climbing the fruit trees and getting the blossoms like they were worms, just to eat something. That's what they did ... eat the blossoms before the fruit came. And we would go in the field to get some green leaves for cooking soup. The really bad period was January through May. We couldn't plant barley or oats in the spring because we didn't have any seed. In the spring, in May, even though the winter wheat was not quite ripe, my father and the boys decided to cut some of it. It was not quite hard enough, but they took what they cut to the mill and we got a sack of flour ... enough to make bread to keep us going until the real harvest. You can't believe how good that tasted! We had enough bread to eat, and we had a cow, so we also had butter. It was delicious.

Fortunately we still had our two colts that we could use as they grew up. My brothers had to take those colts out in the field to graze, as the horses were hungry too, since the grain had been taken away. The horses were so hungry they didn't want to get up, but we helped them to their feet and pulled on their tails to get them out in the field to the grass.

It wasn't until 1924 and 1925 that we finally had some good crops. During this time we were required to deliver some grain to the Communists. The villages came to life again. My brothers Isaac and Peter got married, also my sister Elizabeth, and all lived in Konteniusfeld. My father, Isaac and Peter worked together on both our land and theirs. Isaac had 16 hectares and Peter had 16 hectares, and we did all right again. We had traded our engine for some grain during the famine, but later Isaac and Dad traded a sack of grain for another engine, an even better one. Then in 1927 and 1928 things started to pick up. They didn't take that much of our grain away. We looked to the future and thought it would be all right. Some people bought tractors, and started raising horses again. We had our engine and threshing machine and Isaac and Abe threshed for other people. Later Isaac made a mill from two millstones and milled grain for people in the winter. We started raising crops and raised vegetables, which we took to the villages. Things were looking all right again and then a tragedy occurred in our family.

My mother was a quiet, sincere and hard working person and had lots of patience. But she did not have a very peaceful life. My grandmother, my father's mother, lived with us, which was not good for my mother. Grandmother was jealous, and it was natural, as father was her only son. I can remember that she and my mother often quarreled. But when my brothers Isaac and Peter grew up they stopped it. Mother became ill in 1928, and died of dropsy on September 3, 1928, after being sick for a couple of months. We didn't have doctors in the village at that time like we have here ... I guess it may be better there now. Our villagers had to go very far for a doctor. After mother died, grandmother took over as the 'mother' of the family. It is interesting that after mother died grandmother treated us better ... maybe because she was now in charge. I was about 19 at the time. In 1929 or 1930 my sisters Katherine and Mary married and went to live in eastern Russia in the Amur River region near the China border. When the Amur River was frozen over, people could walk to China and from there they could immigrate to the west. But when my sisters went there the Russians watched that river very closely and they were not able to leave. Now only my father, grandmother, sister Gertrude, brother Abraham, Sara and myself were at home, and we worked our land and Isaac's and Peter's together and did alright.

In 1930 the Communist government started the collectives. Our farmers did not like that they were forced onto the collectives. When you are under the Communists you have to do as you were told or you were sent to Siberia. The Communists used fear tactics ... from every village they took 6 or 7 or more of the best farmers. And they sent these people to Siberia. These were generally the people that had the best farms and were hard working. All their property ... house, farm, and animals went to the collective. When the other people saw what happened to these Kulaks*, meaning those against communism, they naturally agreed to join the collective. There was nothing else for them to do, or else they would lose their property and be sent to Siberia too. The communists also went after preachers and Sunday

----

* Kulak in Russian means a 'fist', indicating both "tightness" of grip and the threat of force. It was a name given to a large class of private land-owning farmers (particularly the more prosperous ones) as socially dangerous, and they were purged in the 1920's and 30's, many being sent to Siberia. (From Encyclopedia Britannica)

school teachers and sent them to prison in Siberia. The churches were used as cow barns, for grain storage, theaters and horse barns. When you passed one of these buildings in the villages you might see a cow or horse looking out a church window! Men in these villages, if they decided in time, would just disappear at night. My brother Isaac had left earlier in 1930 before they got him and found a job in the coke factory in Makeyevka, a 2-day trip by train. He rented a little room there from a nice young Russian couple.

In December 1930 we lost our home and land and everything, because they called my father a "Kulak". We were not for the communist government, but we didn't speak against it, as we were scared to. We all ran away before they could get us. My father went to a Mennonite colony in Memmrick to hide with some friends. Gertrude went to stay with sister Elizabeth, and grandmother went to stay with brother Peter, who was now back in Konteniusfeld and working on the collective. Isaac's wife Mary had stayed temporarily to work on the collective. Isaac had already fled to Makeyevka, so Sara, Abraham and I decided we would 'disappear' to Makeyevka also. We all just disappeared from the village at night … left before they could get us.

Since the communists destroyed all the good farmers and forced the rest into collectives, the collectives did not work well. Not just the city people had starvation, but also the people in the collectives.

3. Makeyevka

In January 1931 Sara, Abe and I fled to the city of Makeyevka, where Isaac had gone a few months earlier. That was before we lost the house in 1930, when he realized what was going to happen. Isaac worked for the Krupps company from Germany ... a big firm that was building a coke factory in Makeyevka. Since he knew both German and Russian, he worked at the factory as an interpreter and also in the library translating books.

We were very lucky to find good jobs in Makeyevka. Makeyevka was an industrial town Northeast of Konteniusfeld with lots of coal mines. It was an act of God that we got jobs there. Isaac and his sister-in-law Liz and I went to a Baptist meeting in someone's house. The churches were closed here too, but some Russian Baptist Christians got together in their small homes to worship and Isaac had joined one of these groups. When the meeting was over, Isaac told us to take the streetcar home and get off at the last station, but the streetcar wasn't running because there was no electricity. So we went back and got Isaac and we started walking home along a street (24ᵗʰ ?) ... it was a long way. On the way we passed a big house and Isaac saw through the window on the windowsill a "fly sprayer" with "fliegen spritze" written on it, so we thought Germans must live there. My brother asked some Russian children playing in the street what kind of house this was and who lives in it. They said "Nimze", meaning Germans. So Isaac said, "Let's go in ... maybe they need some help". Sure enough, after the man heard we spoke both German and Russian, he (Herr Stemmel, the head engineer at the factory) hired us and we started the next morning at 9:00! But Isaac had to falsify our papers (changed "Kulak" to "Srednak" ... meaning "middle farmer") so that it would appear acceptable with the Russians for us to work for the German company. Herr Stremmel told the Russian officers to send these girls (us) to their house to work, so we got jobs. The Germans did not pay us ... it was the Russian government that paid us 75 rubles a month. Some of the other workers were also paid by the Russians. We got a paper or endorsement to say that we were government workers and we got paid from the communist government. Instead of Suzanna, they named me Sophia or Sonja. They called me Sonja and that was in my document too.

We worked in this big house built by the Germans for 31 of their engineers, all from Germany, who worked for the Heinrich-Koppers Co. (from Essen). One room in the house was given to us and we had our meals there too. A Russian girl Maria (Marusa) also lived there with us. This company was building and operating large coke ovens to produce coke, gas and oil from coal. The area around Makeyevka had large amounts of coal. Stalin had arranged for Heinrich-Koppers to come to build up Russia's industry. Since we knew both the German and Russian languages, we were valuable to them. Herr Stemmel, the head engineer, knew Russian very well, but the other engineers didn't know much Russian. They had two cooks, Vera and Sohura, and also 8 girls who did the cleaning. These girls worked in two shifts and none of them knew much German. We worked in the kitchen and served food ... we served the German engineers and acted as interpreters in the kitchen.

Before we came to work in this house, the Germans and the girls had so much trouble understanding each other. Mrs. Jungblut (the chef) would tell Marusa what to buy and what the cook should cook. She would take a piece of paper and draw a fish and would say to Marusa in German this is what we want for dinner ... that's the only way she could communicate. Another engineer had been given a straw pillow, but he wanted a down pillow. He pulled a feather out of another pillow and showing that pillow and the feather to the girl, again in the German language would say "down pillow", so she could understand. And she would say in the Russian language, "how can you expect us to understand you devils". We had lots of laughs there with these girls and the Germans too. It was rather comical you know ... kind of interesting.

Abraham also worked for the Heinrich-Koppers Company. There were thousands and thousands of Russian workers, and he worked there as a mechanic and also as an interpreter. But he really wasn't a good mechanic. Abe made 40 rubles each month, which wasn't much, but you couldn't buy much anyway. He lived in a barracks with about 100 of the workers, and they did not have enough to eat. Abe had a ration card, which got him a little food and he also ate at the dining room sometimes if he had the money. We ate at the German house and got rations too, and were able to give some of them to Isaac, because he didn't make much money. We also helped him out with some food from the Germans.

Abe became very sick a couple of months after we came and the lady doctor who checked him told me he had typhus and wanted to put him in the hospital. I didn't believe her and felt he should go back home, but my brother thought he couldn't make it by himself. I thought Abe was really very lonely in Makeyevka, and that was mostly why he was sick. If he had been put in the typhus barracks, he would have never come out. Brother Isaac asked me to take Abe by train back to our village where brother Peter and sister Elizabeth were and work on the collective.

So I took him to the train station to take him home. In Russia the trains were always two or three hours late, so we had to wait. He decided he wanted to eat, so I took his suitcase and we went to the dining room. It smelled so good ... they served goulash and potatoes and tea. Abe had not eaten very much for days, but there in the dining room I said to myself, "My God, I will never get him out of this place." He ate two helpings of goulash and had three glasses of tea. The Russian custom was to drink tea from glasses. I could see the steam coming up out of the goulash and it smelled so good, but I couldn't eat. I was so nervous for Abe, but he had a ball there at that dining room table. After waiting three hours for the train, we got one and the next day we made it to the station in Stulnjevo, which was 18 kilometers from Konteniusfeld. From there we were able to get a ride to our village. Peter and Elizabeth did not know that we were coming home, and believe me that evening Abe went to see his friends and never laid down ... he was suddenly well ... I just couldn't understand it. I think he had just been sick from loneliness. If Abe had gone to the typhus barracks, I am sure he would not have made it out. I guess Abe was very lonely for home and did not like the life in the city. In the collective they needed workers and Abe stayed in Konteniusfeld and got a job working as a miller. He was about 23, two years older than I was. About this same time Isaac's wife Maria, who had stayed to work on the collective, joined Isaac in Makeyevka.

I stayed at home for two weeks with Elizabeth, and then went back to Makeyevka. And did I ever have a nightmare on the trip. Six miles from Makeyevka there was a stop station and from there we had to get a buggy to go into the city, but we got to the station at 7 o'clock in the evening and no buggies were in sight. So I stayed overnight in that station with 25-30 Russian travelers. There were not enough benches to sit on, and lots of people sat on the floor and some slept. I was sitting on a bench and holding my suitcase tight with my hands and I also fell asleep. All at once I felt somebody loosening up my fingers from my suitcase, and I woke as if lightning had hit me. A young well dressed man 18-20 years old stood in front of me and pretended that he had also fallen asleep and fell right on me. He was very polite and said, "Pardon me, I guess I fell asleep too", and he offered me a cigar. I said no thank you, I do not smoke, and he said, "Oh my you are a proud girl". I did not fall asleep after that, but I watched to see what these 3 young men and one girl did. They robbed the people who were asleep. And those who were watching did not say a word, we were so afraid they would hurt us. This robbery started about midnight and went on until about 3 in the morning. I was scared stiff! In the morning about 7 o'clock, I joined a Russian girl and some men and walked to the city … we did not wait for the buggy. I was so glad to get back to my job again !

Since the communists got rid of all the good farmers and forced the rest into collectives it did not work very well … there was not enough food for the city people or the people in the collectives. We saw so many hungry people in Makeyevka. This was in 1931-1932. The government allowed the Germans and other people from other countries to have special stores, but the poor Russian people couldn't use them. It got so bad that even the people from other countries did not get enough. We couldn't buy much in Makeyevka, but the Germans had a "magezine" (special store). From it they could buy many of the basic things, like clothes, bread, milk and things like that. Also, every month the Heinrich-Koppers firm would send from Germany a food package for each engineer, so they got along much better. And oh, the Germans were very foxy … you know what they did? They had watches sealed inside some of the vegetable cans that came. You could sell the German watches for a pretty good price in Russia. One time Herr Schulte came to me and said, "Sonja (they all called me Sonja), where is my tin of peas?" Herr Schulte was the German engineer that I worked for. I took care of his clothes and things like that … each one of us had so many to take care of … mending and things like that. I figured out that there was something going on and I said, "It's here in the basement". And he said, "I need it, I need it" very secretively, and I realized what was going on. They took the watches out and sold them to the Russian engineers and they made good money!

There were some Russian engineers at the plant, but the Germans did all the commanding. For all the factories built there, there was not one Russian nail or one Russian screw, not even Russian sand, not even Russian brick. It all came from Germany. They said they would not guarantee the work with other country's materials. The Russians had poor material, but in any case, it was good for the German business, you know. But it was a beautiful thing when the factory was ready. It was the second factory they had built in Russia. They also built one in Stalino, which was not too far from Makeyevka. If the war had not come later, they would have built another factory. And they told us that if they built another factory, they wanted us to work for them again.

The working conditions of the Russian workers at the plant were terrible. You have never seen anything like it. There were some girls there just like we were. Their fathers maybe had been good farmers or business people and been called Kulaks. Their property had been taken away like ours, and maybe their fathers and brothers had been sent to Siberia. The girls had fled to the city to look for jobs, just like us. These young girls, beautiful girls, had sacks around their legs and bark from trees to make shoes. They had to carry wooden racks filled with bricks up ladders and pile the bricks for the bricklayers who were building the factory. There were thousands of them, young boys and girls. We could go there, but nobody else could, as those workers had to have numbers and passports. But since we worked for the Germans, the Russians let us see the factory. I felt so sorry for these workers ... the snow and the sleet and the rain, and they had hardly anything to eat. If they had bread (that was the main thing) and could get a glass of milk they felt lucky. They were very poor, very poor. I felt very sorry for them. We had some Russian girls working for us in the house. One was of the same background as we were, but we never talked about it. But we knew, because she said her father used to have horses and things like that. She was a good-looking girl from the Caucasus. Her people, and others who were persecuted, were people like the Mennonites who had money and land ... many of the Russians had money and property. It didn't matter if you were Russian or Mennonite, you could be called a Kulak.

It was while Sara and I were in Makeyevka that my grandmother died in Konteniusfeld ... in 1932 or 1933.

My sister and I, we made money in Makeyevka, but you could not buy much, as the stores were empty. We just got a couple of yards of cotton or flannel and we felt very lucky if we could get a pair of shoes. We could buy at the black market, but the prices were very high. But bodka (vodka) you could always get that in the stores! I worked in Makeyevka for almost three years, from January 1931 to 1933, until the factory was finished and the Germans went home to Germany.

Suzanne at age 23 or 24 in 1932 while she lived and worked in Makeyevka.

Before the Germans left, a German consul came from the city of Kharkov in the Ukraine to visit the factory. His name was Baron Freiherr von Welk and he also did not know Russian. While he was there, realizing the factory would be finished soon, he asked the engineer Herr Brandenbusch if he could take Sara to Kharkov to work as a maid for him. He asked me if it was all right, because she was my younger sister. I said I would be thankful if Sara would get that chance, and that I would somehow find a job there in Makeyevka. He asked if we had ever been separated and I said never. He said he didn't have the right to separate us. But I said, if she is there, maybe later on I can find some work there too. He said I could come too and have a room in his house when it was finished. The Russians were building a house for him across the street from where the General Consul lived. He said he did not have enough work in his house for two, because he didn't get many visitors. However, the general consul across the street from him probably needed help, because he had lots of visitors and needed translators. He said he would give the two of us a room, and when they needed help across the street I could work there.

However, he told us his house in Kharkov was not yet ready, and that in the meantime he had made an arrangement for the two of us to go to another city in the Caucasus to work with a woman who was experimenting with soya beans and other crops. We could stay there and come to Kharkov when his house was ready.

4. In Limbo

When we went to the Caucasus, the plan was to be there just until the consul's house was completed in Kharkov. It took about one and a half or two days to go by train from Makeyevka to the Caucasus. The place we went to was a little town near Kropotkin east of the Azov Sea. I don't remember the name of the town, but we were there for maybe five or six months. We worked on an experimental farm for Fraulein Dr. Miller (Miss Dr. Miller), whom we called "Fraulein Doctor". She was an unmarried German woman who had a doctor's degree and was in charge of an experimental agricultural project. This farm where they did the experiments had once been the farm of a rich Russian family, which had been sent to Siberia, and now it belonged to the government. And what a beautiful house and place it had been.

Over a hundred kinds of soya were being grown there and Dr. Miller herself had picked many different kinds of soya in India and other countries. She was cross-pollinating the different types of soya to get better ones. We had to be so careful when we sorted them out that the beans did not get mixed. The Indian soya plants were only maybe five inches high, while the others were a foot high, two feet high, maybe even 5 feet high. She made different things from the beans: flour, oil, and cocoa butter, and would grow them in little light to make salad greens from the leaves. It was very good protein. She also planted peanuts and the Russians had never ever seen a peanut.

While we were there, we lived in rooms upstairs above the dining room. He (the consul) paid for our room and our board. It was a very nice experience. But then one day we were called into the office, where the director of this experimental farm said that he had recently been to Germany and to Leningrad where he had met Baron Freiherr von Welk. He was awfully sorry to tell us that the Baron could not take us right now. He had been transferred from Kharkov to Leningrad, but could not hire us in place of the cook and the girl who had been at the house for over ten years. They practically belonged to that house. He said we should go back to our village, Konteniusfeld, that he had our address and he would look for a place for us in Leningrad. He gave us (Sara and me) 1000 German marks (500 each) and some food for our trip home to Konteniusfeld. My sisters Elizabeth and Gertrude, and brothers Peter and Abe now lived there, as did my father with sister Elizabeth.

While we were waiting for the train at the station, a well-dressed Russian man came in, checked his suitcase and came to our table and asked if he could sit down. We said alright, but we were suspicious of him. We had our suitcases with us (between our legs under the table for safety). Being a very nervous person, I was always getting up to check when the train was coming. You know the trains were always late, and when they came in there was always a big rush to get a seat. When it finally did come in, we got up to get in line but he said to sit down and wait. We couldn't understand it … we thought we wouldn't get a seat, but he said not to worry. After all the other people were on the train (and the train overfilled) he called the conductor who came with his lantern and the Russian told him to open "this" car. We got in (a passenger car) and said goodbye to him (he took another train) and we had the whole car ... 30 or 40 seats all to ourselves. Every 15 minutes or so, the conductor would come with his lantern and check on us. After a while we heard soldiers get into the next car and we were a bit afraid, but they stayed there. Apparently the Russian man had asked the conductor to make sure we were safe. He maybe thought we were from Germany. He had told us in the station that he was going to tell the government that the trains were a mess. He was very nice and friendly. He must have been a "big shot" to get us that car all to ourselves.

When we came home we joined the collective again. That was in the autumn of 1933. My sister Elizabeth and her husband, my brother Peter and his wife and my brother Abe were there on the collective. Gertrude and my father stayed with Elizabeth, and Grandmother stayed with Peter. Abe wasn't married, but worked on the collective. Sara had met David Hebert, a bookkeeper, in Makeyevka and about a year after we returned to Konteniusfeld they got married there. They returned to Makeyevka.

The people like us, Kulak's children and also the minister's daughters, Katherine and Anna Bolt who were about 45 years old, had to do the dirtiest and hardest work on the collective and there was no pay. Each village was made into a collective, each having a Burgermeister (mayor or head), but now he served the government. He had to make sure that there was order and that we worked hard so that the collective would produce more and send as much as possible to the cities. Our Burgermeister was Abraham Schartner, who was a pretty good mayor but he had to do some things that the people didn't like, because he was forced to from higher up. The Schartners were poorer than we were. They farmed also, but also worked for other farmers. So they were not Kulaks, and being from a poorer background he became Burgermeister, but he was a hard worker and really did like collectives.

One Saturday afternoon, during the summer after working all day, and all week and looking forward to getting cleaned up and having a rest, Henry Durksen told us that two people, Liz (Isaac's sister-in-law) and I should get ready to go to another collective to work. Henry Durksen was secretary or something like that in the collective. His father had been a blacksmith and had done pretty well, but when I was young he went bankrupt and lost his business. After that they got 16 hectares of land and started farming. During the civil war, when the Reds and Whites were fighting back and forth around our village, young Henry was for the Reds. So later on he fit into the collective very well.

Anyway, we got washed up and got some clothes and a blanket and that afternoon about 4 or 5 o'clock a truck came with two armed soldiers to pick us up. They went from village to village (eight villages) picking up 2 to 4 people at each, so that about 20 of us were on the truck when we got to the "colcos" ... not really a village collective, but some government land. There were a few mud huts filled with green hay to sleep on, and a "kukna" (kitchen) with some outside tables where we ate. The food was often bad, so we also bought a little bread and milk from a Russian woman that lived there. All the time that I was there we "chased bugs". Liz and I would stretch a long rope between us and walk through the wheat to knock off the bugs. We probably did more damage than the bugs! In the evening we all got together (no lights, no electricity, just moonlight) and sang folk songs. Then we would go to sleep on the green hay in the huts. We could only take a sponge bath with a pail of water.

After about a month I got very sick and couldn't work because of chest pains. They called a doctor who told me I had pneumonia. The doctor was one of us, had a Mennonite name, and I asked if he would write a note to our Russian boss that I couldn't work. With that, I asked the boss if I could go home. So I walked home ... it was about 40 to 50 kilometers, and I walked all day, getting home after dark. I was in a lot of pain and often thought I wouldn't make it, but never sat down, as I knew I would not get up again. After a few days at home, I walked to Gnadenfeld to see a doctor who gave me some medicine and a paper that said I had "tuberculosis".

5. Leningrad

In 1934, a year after leaving Kropotkin, we got a telegram from the Baron. He had found a nice place for Sara and me in Leningrad and asked us to send him a wire immediately if we could come. I wired him that Sara had gotten married and couldn't go, but that I could come. So I took the train to Leningrad from the Stulnjevo station (18 km from Konteniusfeld), a trip that took three days, and resulted in me being away from home for seven years. A group of students from Leningrad, who had been vacationing on the Black and Azov seas, were also on the train and I got to know them. They wanted to know what University I went to. I told them I was going to visit a friend, not to a university, and they were interested where I would be staying, but I didn't tell them. They were interested that I spoke German and broken Russian and I think they thought I was from Germany.

The train arrived in Leningrad at 6 in the morning and I waited in the station until 9 o'clock, praying all the time that I would be lucky enough to get a good job. Then I hired a man to accompany me on a streetcar to the German consulate. When I got there the police (Russian) asked me who I wanted to see (they were always suspicious and nosy) and I said I wanted to visit the "cook". I rang the bell, the gate opened and I went into the kitchen. There the cook showed me the bathroom, where I could bathe and clean up before I saw the consul.

I went to Baron von Welk's room and told him again that Sara could not come because she had gotten married. He asked me, "To a Russian or a German?" and I said, "A German bookkeeper", and he said he approved! He also asked about the 1000 marks. I told him about how Isaac had gone to the "torksin", a store for foreigners, and they told Isaac the marks were not worth anything, but would not give them back ... they stole them from Isaac.

He then told me the situation in Leningrad ... that he couldn't take me himself, because the cook and his maid had been there over 10 years. However, he had found a place in an English home, the home of a Lady Muriel Paget.

Lady Muriel* was the good-will ambassador for King George V (the current Queen Elizabeth's grandfather). All the linen: sheets, towels, tablecloths, blankets and pillows had the English crown. They had many visitors and I served at the table and acted as an interpreter. I didn't really know very much English, but I could understand her well enough to tell the cook and chauffeurs what she wanted. There were around 60 'English'

----
* The following is a summary from a Wikipedia article ...
  http://en.wikipedia.org/wiki/Muriel_Paget Ref. 12.

Lady Muriel had spent several years providing humanitarian aid in London beginning in 1905, and she then worked in several Eastern European countries, including Russia, during and after WW I. She left Russia during the period when England broke diplomatic relations with Russia (Soviet Union) after the revolution.

After diplomatic relations resumed, she returned to Leningrad in 1930. There were a number of "Displaced British Subjects" (DBSs) living in Russia and Lady Muriel returned to provide basic assistance to them. (These persons and the support they received are largely as Suzanne describes.) Lady Muriel established a 'British Subjects in Russia Relief Organization' in Britain through which funds were raised.

Lady Muriel presumably left Russia in the late 1930's and died in 1938. In 1938 there was a trial in Russia of a former Soviet ambassador who admitted he had spied for Britain at the request of Lady Muriel Paget. The issue was later debated at length in the British Parliament. Prime Minister Chamberlain claimed she was not involved with the British Intelligence Service, but others claimed she was. (So Suzanne was likely correct about her suspicions of Lady Muriel's activities.)

families that lived in Leningrad and had English passports and were British subjects. They got help from Lady Muriel: money and material that were brought over from England. I asked Miss Healey, the secretary, how it was that these people hardly knew a word of English, but were British subjects. I could not understand this. She said that many years earlier it was quite easy to become a British subject. People went to the British consul and told them that they had some distant relative in England, and that they would like to become English citizens. Many did and they got British passports. They didn't have that much English blood in them, I'm sure of that. But they were glad to get the money every month.

Lady Muriel had a doctor and a dentist for all these people that called themselves English, and she had three chauffeurs to help with her duties. The doctor was Doctor Bell, who I didn't like. The dentist was a Jewish lady from Leningrad. All the "British subjects" and the people that worked for Lady Muriel got free treatment and material from England.

For a month's work she paid me 40 rubles in Russian money, and two and a half English shillings. For one shilling I could get forty rubles. You could trade shillings to the Russian people for rubles, because they could use the English money to buy things at the "torksin", a store operated by the communists. One could buy things there with gold or silver, but they did not take Russian rubles.

The people from the consulates (other countries) bought all of their food there. The food and the goods at the torksin were of very good quality, but you couldn't buy much that was very good with Russian money at the regular stores. Some Russian people would trade their last silver or gold jewelry to get things they could not find at regular stores. Some wanted certain foods, maybe cocoa or rice for a sick baby or child. That's how the communist government 'fished' all the gold and silver from the Russian people, and also the dollars (shillings) from the consulates.

Gena, later my husband, was the first man I met when I went to meet Lady Muriel. She lived and had her offices in the Swedish consul building. On one side of this building there were Germans on the first story, Danish people on the second, Lady Muriel on the third and on the top floor more Germans. On the other side of the building were the Swedish and Finnish consulates. Theodore Stelzig, later my father-in-law, worked for the Swedish consulate, but he served all of the consulates. Gena's sister Eleanor also worked for the Swedish consulate. Gena's brother Arthur and Eleanor lived with their father and mother, who had a free apartment because they worked there. Gena had a room in Leningrad (in the city), but would regularly come to visit his family.

Arthur and Gena were mechanics (precision machinists) and were fairly highly skilled people in the Russian factories. Gena worked for a big factory called 'Bolshevik'. He was a specialist (precision machinist) and there were maybe only thirty or forty like him, something like that, at Bolshevik. They were not paid by the hour there. The Communists did not believe in paying by the hour ... the machinists were paid by the piece. If you were quick and good you made more money. It was up to you. Gena said that sometimes the pieces would only be a "hair" off and the inspectors would call them "brach" (not good), and he wouldn't get credit for them.

I went with Gena for about a year before we got married. Our courtship, it was fun and he liked fun. He never complained of being tired from work. We went to the theater, to the opera, to the museums, and to the Peterhof (the summer place where Peter the Great had lived), which was kept as a museum with the Tsarina's dresses, the Tsar's furniture and other things. And we went boating. I was scared of boating, but Gena made me go. We had lots of fun outside and they had beautiful parks in Leningrad. In the summertime the parks were full of people. The courtship was quite informal. He would take me to a show or to the theater or the opera, and then we would come home and go to his parents and have a cup of tea with the whole family. The family was very close. The father and sons and daughter were like friends. They would share everything with their parents, except sometimes things that would worry mother, they would keep from her, but would tell dad. They all spoke four languages - Finnish, German, Russian and Swedish. Father didn't speak Swedish well, even though he worked for the Swedish consul. He spoke mainly German and Russian and a little bit of Finnish. Ella (Eleanor) interpreted books in the other languages, and spoke Finnish and Swedish where she worked, but my husband and Arthur didn't speak the other languages as fluently as Eleanor.

We had been going together almost a year when Gena proposed to me. We were in Lady Muriel's apartment, and I wasn't really surprised. I thought he would sooner or later, and I was happy ... I liked the whole family. After he proposed he said, "Let's go tell dad and mom". I didn't like to do that, as I was kind of shy. He didn't get me a ring, but his mother gave him a ring to give me. (Many years later in 1970, when I visited my Arthur and Evelyn, I gave the ring to Evelyn, because it was from Gena's mother. I said, "Arthur, I want it in your family.") Gena's parents were very happy. They liked me and I liked the family very much. Gena had not met my family in Konteniusfeld and never did.

We were married October 28, 1935 in a church ... in the Petrich Church (Peter's Church). This was not St. Peter's, but was named after Peter the Great. Peter's Church was a very large Lutheran Church, and Gena's family was Lutheran. There were only a few churches open in Leningrad. The Communists kept these open only so that people from other countries would not think that they didn't have any. I don't know why they allowed us to be married in a church. Just Gena's family and some of my friends that had come from the Ukraine to work in Leningrad came to the wedding. Also, some of Gena's relatives, as well as the bookkeeper (Mr. Sanders), Lady Muriel's secretary (Miss

33

Healey) and Mrs. Morley attended. Mrs. Morley was responsible for the whole household when Lady Muriel was gone.

Lady Muriel wanted very much to be at our wedding, but she had to go to Japan to visit her daughter. She had a daughter there whose husband was an ambassador and another daughter whose husband was an ambassador in China. She was planning to be home, but something happened and she couldn't come.

Suzanne and Gena on their wedding day, October 28, 1935.

Lady Muriel had wanted us to have the reception in her apartment, and we told Gena's parents. At that time I didn't know that my father-in-law was a spy for the Communists. He was forced to be, and only after his death did we find out. He was told that if he wanted his children to be happy they shouldn't

34

have the reception in that English house. My father-in-law had a communist friend, so we arranged to have the reception in his apartment. I guess he was not a bad one, because he let us have our wedding dinner there.

So, after the wedding we were chauffeured to the reception by Lady Muriel's chauffeur. I didn't know anything about cars then, but it was a brand new white car, and she had insisted that we use that car. The apartment houses had long halls with many rooms (apartments) on either side, one door after another. I had a veil ... a bridal veil, and during the reception I wanted to go to the washroom, and the man's wife came with me and she looked both ways so no one would see me in the veil, as a veil was a part of religious tradition, which the communists didn't like. For dinner we had herring, cold cuts of meat, potato salad, wine, beer, tea and later some sweet stuff like cake. But there was no wedding cake.

I'd had wine before. At Lady Muriel's a little glass of vodka was served as a before-dinner drink. Sir Richard, her husband, liked the way we served vodka. We put some grated orange peel and a little sugar in it, and he just loved it. For dinner there would usually be one meat course and one fish course, so there would be a glass of red wine and also a glass of white wine served. Lady Muriel was the one who served at the table. She would serve very small portions of both food and wine. The British consul, Glade Smith, would say to his cook, "Put something in the stove for later, because we're going to Lady Muriel's".

After the wedding dinner we went to Gena's place. We had to travel about 25 minutes by trolley bus to get there. We didn't have any vacation or honeymoon, except just going to his place. But Mrs. Morley told me I didn't need to come to work for four days.

I continued to work for Lady Muriel and Gena continued working as a machinist. Gena and I had a one-room apartment. In Russia then all that most people could get was a one-room apartment. We had a big room and were very fortunate to have it. You made a partition and you would have a bedroom and a living room, and that's where you lived. We had clothes closets, good ones. There was a common kitchen where everyone on our floor of the building cooked together. This was a building some people had owned, and the communists had taken it over. The people who had owned this building were very lucky, because they were allowed to stay in the building after it was taken from them. But they just had two rooms, and the other rooms were given to other people. It was a four-story house. On our floor there was a hall and on both sides were rooms and then at one end there was the kitchen and the "bathroom" ... not a real bathroom, just a toilet. You'd go to the city about once a week where there was a bathhouse. You had to pay there and that's where you took a bath. At home you took a sponge bath, that's all you had. There were four families using the kitchen. Each had its own table in a corner of the kitchen, and each had their own pots and pans and dishes. We had a little gas stove (we called it a 'primus') and that's what we cooked on. They didn't have gas stoves like we have here. Each week the cleaning of the hall and kitchen was done by one of the families. There were no problems, never a fight. Everyone knew what to do. You would be surprised how you cooperate when you have to.

Every summer we would leave the city and go to Pudis in the country where there was a nice lake and summer homes. Lots of Finns lived there and Gena would rent a house there. He would get three weeks for holidays and he would also come weekends. We would go there by train ... about a one-hour ride. I stayed there for three months during the summer, every summer, and he would come there weekends.

We would go to the opera and plays, but would go to a show only when there was a very good show. I remember I went to one movie three times, and that was a German movie, "De Kleine Mama" (The Little Mama). It was so beautiful and so good that I went three times to that. Most of them were war movies, and I didn't go for that. But to the theater and the opera, we went often.

Suzanne and Gena in the country, during winter.

Gena's family had a very bad experience some years earlier. My father-in-law had been a chief-of-police in Leningrad before the communists had taken over. He had to run away because they wanted to put him in prison or kill him. He escaped to the country and hid. His wife had to move out of Leningrad. A friend of hers said to her, "Well, Olga Adamovna, you have to leave now or they will come and get you." So she took just her silver and gold and went over the Neva Bridge to the city of Ostrov, and hid there among her friends. The city of Ostrov is an island, which is connected to Leningrad by bridges. She hid there with friends and later went into the country where her husband was. Her husband hid in the timber and would come in

37

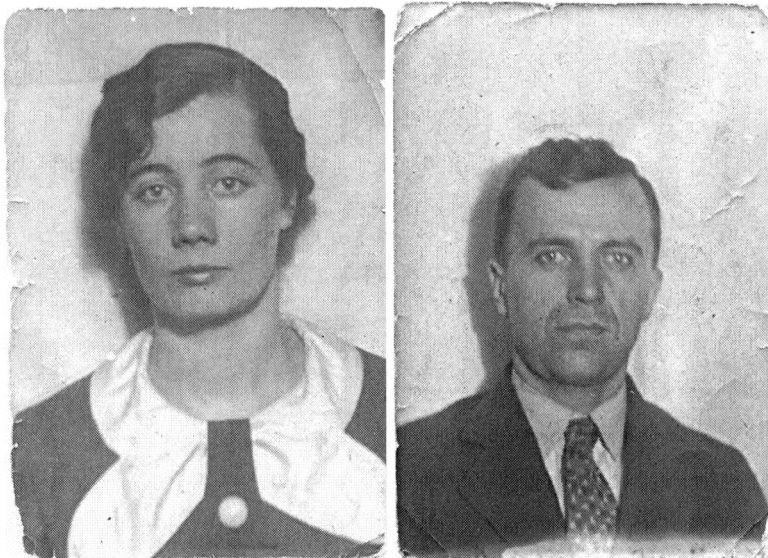

Photos of Suzanne and Gena. These were likely taken in Leningrad sometime after they married (between 1936 and 1941). On the back of each of these photos is the label of a Stuttgart firm in Germany. Presumably Suzanne had saved smaller pictures of her and Gena (maybe passport or identification photos) and after escaping to West Germany had them copied. Note the frayed edges, no doubt due to the wear and tear during her travail.

the night and get some food from her. Gena was alone in Leningrad and was trying to keep the apartment. It was beautiful, with Persian rugs and good furniture. He worked as a machinist for a couple which still had their own shop. They wanted him to marry their granddaughter. He was trying to keep the apartment, so father and mother could come back to live in it sometime later. But the communists threw him out. So he moved in with these elderly people and worked for them. Then somehow he became connected with the Swedish consul, which was looking for a girl. That's how he got his sister Ella back to Leningrad. She worked for the Swedish consul. Later the Swedish consul needed a man like their father, and that's how Gena's father came back after several years and worked in Leningrad with these people. After a long enough period, the communists had sort of forgotten. I have read some letters that Gena's mother gave me to read ... how Gena had written about how cold it had been, how his feet were frozen, and he worked so hard. He worked so hard after they had lost everything. He said sometimes he would like so much to have an ice cream, but he saved his pennies for his father and mother and sent them the money. And he eventually got them all back to Leningrad.

My father-in-law Theodore Stelzig died in 1936. When he died mother told us, "Now I will tell you, the NKVD called him and asked him to spy on the whole house where you work, on the Finnish, the Swedish, the British and the Germans. Theodore was in a good place to watch these people, because they all had to go through that part of the house where his desk was. The NKVD wanted to know where the guests came from, what their reasons were for coming and things like that. That's what he was to find out and tell them. If he would tell anybody that he was spying, they would shoot him. He was to come twice a week in the evening (it was not very far from where we lived) to the house where the NKVD was located. He said to them, "What do you think this will do to my wife, when she knows I'm going out twice a week in the evening and I don't tell her where I'm going. My wife will be broken-hearted". So then they asked him if she could keep a secret, and he said that she could. So they said he could tell her, but nobody else. So she was the only one that knew he was a spy until after he died ... when she told the family.

She said that they had been really very reasonable with him. Well, naturally if my father-in-law really knew something suspicious, he never would say anything anyway. I'm sure that the chauffeurs were spies. They (NKVD) had also asked my father-in-law about "that" girl (me) who was with Lady Muriel. They knew where I was from, since when I came the NKVD had of course seen my passport. They knew practically everything. They asked him if he thought I was reliable ... if I would not talk.

He said he thought I wouldn't talk, but he said, "You know that girl is sick." He meant I was not too stable mentally. He was protecting me. I am so glad. They wanted me to spy at the table on Lady Muriel and the guests from other countries, and let them know what was going on, but since I wasn't 'right' they didn't ask me. You would not believe how suspicious everyone was of everyone else in Russia. When my father-in-law came up to Lady Muriel's apartment to ask for my passport when I first came to Leningrad, I had a feeling then that he was a spy.

When my father-in-law died in 1936, the Swedish consul asked Arthur if he would take father's job (that would give the family the apartment again). The apartment and rooms were so rare in Russia you have no idea. So Arthur took the job in the Swedish consul because of his mother. But there was a Russian fellow who wanted the job. He was one of two cleaning men, who brought wood into each apartment of the consul house and did the cleaning. He thought he was capable of having Arthur's job, but he wasn't, he didn't have the education. He was jealous of Arthur, and this fellow got Arthur's job, apparently by telling the NKVD something bad about Arthur. We all were very sure it was him, because he came home so drunk the night they came to take Arthur away. We went to the lawyers and we paid lots of money to them to find out something, but you could not believe them. They said things like, your brother is alive and he works somewhere, but he doesn't know what his neighbor does. Each does his secret work. It could be, I don't know if it was true or not. We paid the lawyers, because Arthur was innocent and we wanted to get him back, but we never saw or heard from him again.

In 1939, the 20th of June, our son Arthur was born and my goodness were the Stelzigs ever proud of him. I said to my mother-in-law, "I don't know if you will ever see a second son, so I want you to name him". And she said, because her son Arthur had been taken away, she would like him to be named Arthur.

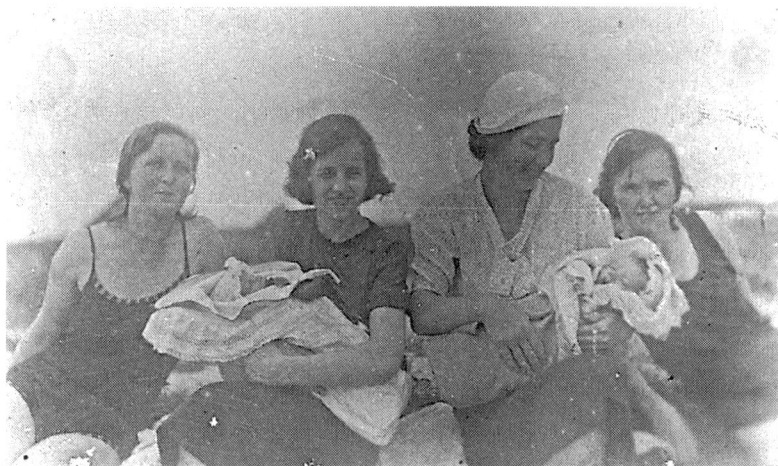

Suzanne with Arthur a few months old, pictured with another mother and
child and two other women. One of the 'other' women is
very likely Suzanne's sister-in-law Ella.

Gena with Arthur, and Arthur on blanket (Arthur about 1 year old).

41

Gena's mother said if you don't mind, I want my "Arthur" back, and I said that's fine, and so she named my son Arthur. And Ella, you know she was crazy about him. Ella had insured herself, and if something happened to her, the money was to go to Gena, but when Arthur was born she changed it to Arthur.

Arthur was an awfully good boy. When the doctor came to check him (my mother-in-law was often sick and I stayed in the house and took care of her), she would say, "You don't know how lucky you are to have a baby like that". Arthur was a really good baby. What got in him later, I don't know! ☺

Sadly, "mother" (Gena's mother) died in 1940 from dropsy, just like my mother in 1928. Arthur was not yet two.

6. An Extended 'Vacation'

In 1941 Gena and I made plans to go to the Ukraine to visit my family. If Gena's mother had not died, we probably would not have decided to go. My husband had never seen the Ukraine, and my family had never seen Gena or Arthur. I wished that we would all go together, but a fellow my husband worked with, who was a Communist but had been good to Gena, said to him, "Why don't you let your wife go out of Leningrad, out of the city air, to where the fresh air is." He said, "Later on you can go, as we are not sure you will get your holiday right away." So Gena came home and told me and I said, "I hate to go alone, but alright." So then I went to the doctor for a check-up for Arthur. The lady doctor said to me, "I really could stop you from going, because the atmosphere here and in the Ukraine are so different he could get very sick there. But I will give him some medicine and maybe then you can go."

The train we went on had a sleeper so we traveled very nicely. Gena and Eleanor both came to the train and Gena said, "This is the way I will come. I will take a sleeper too." This was June 19, 1941. Then I said to him, "Gena, you know I have a feeling that I will never see you again." And he said, "Why do you think of that?" Well, I said, "I just don't know, I just feel it." I don't know why, I just said it. He said, "I will be there in maybe three weeks, maybe a month."

It took three days and three nights to travel to the Ukraine from Leningrad by train. When we arrived in Konteniusfeld on Sunday, my sisters had already heard over the radio that the war had broken out. I didn't know a thing about it yet. While we were on the train Germany had declared war on the Soviet Union, but the train people did not tell us! We arrived on June 22, 1941, and in the afternoon Elizabeth came and said, "Suzanne, we don't want to scare you, but war is on." And I said, "With whom?" and she said, "With Germany." I said, "They

43

cannot win ... the Russians have a good army ... they cannot win, Germany is too little for that."

After that I could not write to my husband in the German language. I had to write in Russian. When Gena sent me his first telegram with 500 rubles and asked me to come home, I couldn't. Arthur was very sick from the change, just too hard for a little boy to take I guess. The doctor had told me so. So I sent a telegram back, "Arthur sick, cannot come right now." Then I got another telegram with 1000 rubles and again he asked me to come home. Then he sent me 500 rubles with the third telegram and asked me to stay where I was. He said all the children, babies and mothers from Leningrad were being sent for safety to Siberia, because it looked bad for Leningrad. He said I was better off with my sisters than all alone somewhere in Siberia. After that there was no more news ... I never heard from him again. That third telegram was the last I heard from Gena, about one or two months after arriving in the Ukraine, when he sent me the 500 rubles.

A few years later in East Germany, I asked some Russian soldiers what had happened to that big 'Bolshevik' factory, and they told me the whole factory and the workers were sent east to Siberia. Oh, then I thought my husband could be alive, because they needed him for work. But if he couldn't get out, he couldn't be alive. The Russian soldiers told me that food was so scarce later in Leningrad that cats and rats and mice were being sold in the markets. People might trade a Persian lamb coat for a sack of potatoes and many burned their furniture to heat their rooms. It was terrible, and the starvation was terrible. They had ration cards and got new ones each month. But if people living in a house knew that one of them in the house died and it was in the middle of the month, they wouldn't let the authorities know that the person was dead ... they left him there and used his rations for the rest of the month.

After the war broke out, Stalin issued orders that all those with German names were to be destroyed, sent away to Siberia or something like that. The men from 16 years old to 65 or 68 were sent away, not by car, not by horses or wagons, but by walking. They were herded like animals. The police rode beside with guns. Some people that had seen them being herded away by the police said the policemen could not understand these people. They knew that they would die but they sang, "Nearer My God to Thee", and the Russian policemen just didn't know what to think about that. The people knew what would happen to them, but they still could sing a hymn.

My brother-in-law, Henry Kasper; my nephew, Hans, who was Peter and Walter's older brother; and my sister Mary's husband, Abraham Edieger, were all taken away. My brothers, Isaac, Peter and Abraham had been taken away in 1937 or 1938 while I was in Leningrad. I don't know why they were taken. The police would just come in the night and take some men from here and some from there. Everyone was prepared for it. In Leningrad I had prepared my husband's clothes ... my husband's winter clothes, because he would need warm underclothes for Siberia. They were all safe in the drawer, so that if he was taken in the night, the clothes would be ready. Because I knew I would never have a chance to give them to him. And I always kept them there, just in case. And that's what the police did, they went from village to village taking the men away. It was so easy. If someone didn't like you, they could just go to the police and say you were for the Germans. That was enough. You had to go, and you had nothing to say about it. So, the last time I saw my three brothers was in 1934 before I went to Leningrad.

The women and the children of the men who were taken away were looked on as enemies too. They didn't get good jobs. My sister-in-law Suzanne (Peter's wife) was pregnant with her seventh child, and she had to work to make a living after Peter was taken away. It was a lot different if your husband was home, than if your husband was taken away. After the last of the grown men were taken away to Siberia in 1941, all the women and children had to work on the collectives.

So Arthur and I lived in Konteniusfeld with what was left of my family. Later on, they also started shipping the women and children away, so they would not fall into the hands of the Germans. One morning in October 1941, not long before we were overrun by the German army, Russian soldiers ordered us to the Stulnjevo railroad station to be shipped east. When we got to the station we saw with our own eyes people from the Crimea going by in open cars. And they said, "We saw the Germans coming, but we had to leave. And we know where we are going ... to Siberia" ... it was late October and they went in open cars !

There were about 7000 of us at the Stulnjevo railroad station ... 7000 people! There was a man doctor, and you know how he was with us? He wore women's clothes and hardly anybody knew that he was a doctor from Halbstadt. And others had done the same thing ... they saved themselves from being taken away by wearing women's clothes. That's how they had not been sent away earlier. Children were born there, snow was falling there, and people died there too, the old ones. They even took the sick people who had been in bed for months. We were all out in the open field waiting for the train to pick us up. But it didn't happen! There was this man who was the director of the railroad station. He told some of our leaders that we were too close to the railroad track, but he didn't explain why, he just wanted us to move back away from the track. So we started to pull our sacks, our food, and everything we had been able to take with us away from the tracks, and then lay down to sleep. And all at once, BOOM ! BOOM! My goodness, now we thought they (the Germans) were here and were shooting at us. But this man had blown up the tracks so that no trains could go through.

Then suddenly we heard machine guns but we didn't know what was happening. Soon a plane crashed and was burning. There was a Russian woman in our group who had lived with the Mennonites, so she was "guilty" too and also had to go. She was so brave. She ran and pulled the pilot out of the plane and got his papers. She knew exactly who he was and where he came from because of his passport and papers. And do you know what the papers said? They were instructions to destroy all the people there at the station, because they had not been shipped away. The papers said he was from Moscow and this plane was sent to kill us there. But a German airplane shot him down before he could do it. Can you believe it? What a close call ! Later, after the Germans overran us and found out that the station director had saved 7000 lives, they gave him a car and a watch ... they paid him well.

We had to stay there at the station, as we felt like prisoners. Then someone realized that our Russian guards had just disappeared! But we didn't know how to get home ... our village was 18 km away and we had no horses, nothing. But then people found a horse here and a horse somewhere else and slowly we, the women, children and old men that had been herded to the station, slowly managed to make their way back to their villages.

47

7. Home Again

When they took us to the station to ship us out, the Russians remaining in our area could do what they wanted with our stuff, because we would not be coming back. When we did come home you would not believe it. They had used our potato patch in the basement as a toilet. So we didn't eat anything that was left, as you never knew what had happened to it. My nephew Henry's dog and pigeons were hanging out on a string, dead. The cows were gone, and the pigs were gone. My sister had hives of bees and the bees had been destroyed by pouring boiling water on them. They had tried to destroy most of what we had. The people (the Russians) were told to put kerosene on the buildings and burn them. There were good Russians there too, but they got their orders and they were afraid not to obey them. But some of our Mennonite women who got home first pleaded with them not to burn their homes and their furniture. So the villages were not badly burned, but if we had come just a half-day later the buildings would have been in flames. And that's how we found it when we came home. We got some straw and slept on the floor.

Then we started to get things together again, and we had to go to work in the collective again. We got a different mayor for our village, and we started to work and things were not too bad. It is amazing how quickly we could get started again.

The Germans had been stopped for quite a while at the Dnieper River to the west, but when they crossed the Dnieper, they overran the Ukraine very quickly. It was not long before the Germans overran us. There wasn't much fighting right around us, but we heard some thunder (explosions) far away. We were afraid to talk ... always afraid of what might happen. Some Russian soldiers came and moved in, but they were good. They wished that they could hide there in the village. They didn't want to fight in the war. One fellow came to my father and asked if he could hide somewhere near us. But father couldn't do that. He told the man that if he wanted he could go hide somewhere near and he would not tell anybody. One basement was found full of Russian soldiers, like herring in a basket, and they fought among themselves for a plum stone to eat. Nobody knew they were there. When the Germans came, these soldiers came out with their hands up and gave up. But the SS didn't treat them very well. If they had treated the Russians better, many of the Russians would have surrendered earlier and would have been willing to help them, but they got bad treatment from the Germans. First came the German motorcycles ... whether they were SS or what they were, I don't know. We had never seen anything like it. The poor Russian soldiers were so poorly clothed, and here come these dressy motorcycle riders and we were scared. But they heard us talking German and they said, "You speak German?" We said, "Yes". Oh my goodness, we were their best friends then.

I cannot say the German soldiers did any harm where we were. After we were overrun, we had three or four SS men stay with us. Each family had some. There was Wachman, oh he was a bad one. One was the son of an ambassador who had lived in Moscow, and he spoke the Russian language quite well. He was good. But Wachman was a beast. There was another one and he was a beast too. I didn't like them. They wanted us to say "Heil Hitler" and things like that, but I never did that. One time a girl came into the office where Wachman was and she didn't say "Heil Hitler". I think he asked her to say "Heil Hitler" and she maybe refused him. And he took out his "gummy" belt, and I tell you she got it. But that didn't do any good ... people hated them for that.

Then there was the big battle of Leningrad*, which was

----

*   Suzanne says on next page that she didn't know what happened to Gena in Leningrad, but Arthur recalls her receiving a Red Cross letter while they were in Pincher Creek, indicating Gena did not survive the siege. See p. 93.

49

surrounded by the Germans in late 1941 and cut off for over two years ... more than two entire winters. My poor Gena was possibly in Leningrad during its siege, or maybe he had been shipped out to Siberia, I don't know. After the Germans overran us in the Ukraine, there was the big battle of Stalingrad (Volgograd), which was east of us on the Volga River. After a six months long battle to take Stalingrad, starting in fall of 1942, the Germans were not able to and they began to retreat. We were quite a way west of Stalingrad ... maybe 300 or 400 miles. In the fall of 1943 we were told to leave because the Russians were advancing and this was to be a terribly difficult journey for us!

8. The Trek

Because the Germans were retreating back from Stalingrad and the Russians would be soon overrunning our villages, we were told by these German SS fellows that we would have to leave. That's when we had to form a wagon train and move west. But here again was a trick by those SS fellows. The SS was responsible for taking us out of Russia, but they let us sit until the last minute and then they told us to get out. If these SS fellows got us back to Germany too soon, they would lose this safe and easy "job" of "guarding" us. It was an easier and safer job to boss us around than to be at the front with their retreating army. If they took us quickly to Germany, where we should have gone right away, then they would lose this good job and would be sent to the front to fight in the war where they should have been!

When we started in October of 1943 it was rainy weather and they always just kept us a little ahead of the fighting. In the late 1930's and just after the war started, the Communists had taken all the grown men from our village, including my brothers Isaac, Peter, and Abraham, and the husbands of my sisters and some of my older nephews. So we had no men to help us, only my father who was seventy-three and four of my young nephews. Arthur was only four years old. In the wagon train there were my sister Elizabeth and her three children (Henry, Elizabeth and Maria), my father, my sister Gertrude, Mary with her children (Mary and Henri), Sara with her child (Nelda), me with my boy Arthur, and also my sister-in-law Mary with her children Peter and Walter. Arthur and I were with Elizabeth in her wagon. Peter and Walter were young boys. Peter and Henri were about the same age, about 16 years old, and Walter was a little younger, about 15 years old. And they had to take care of so many wagons because we had no grown men. There were many, many wagons in the train, and there were Mennonites, non-Mennonite Germans and some Russians. There were some Russian people

51

who wanted to get out and they were also in the trek. They still had their men, but we did not.

This picture* is from a Mennonite resource of the "Trek" from the Southern Ukraine (Konteniusfeld and other Mennonite communities) to the Polish border during the late fall-winter of 1943. This is early in the "Trek" when they still had all their horses and cows. Later in the trek, most of the livestock succumbed due to lack of food and the cold and wet. Suzanne is the woman in the dark coat walking beside the cow. Her sister-in-law Maria is driving the wagon. Arthur is likely in another wagon ... Elizabeth's. The other woman walking (light coat) is unknown. In looking at many of the other pictures in this resource on the Trek, it is interesting that one sees only women and children. All the able bodied men had been taken away in the 1930's and early 40's to unknown locations to the east, most likely to labor camps east of the Urals. This picture, of which there are several on the Mennonite site, appeared on the cover of a book describing the Trek, "Gedenk Buechlein" (in German) by P.H. Dirks, and published June 1951. See footnote on next page. Picture purchased from Ref. 7, and used with permission.

There were maybe a thousand wagons in the train ... it stretched for miles. It took about three months (to get to the Polish border), but we didn't travel all the time. When it sounded a little better (the fighting) they would stop us. We didn't hear any news, we didn't have any newspapers, and we didn't have any radios. We had to do what the SS men told us to do. Of course the SS men went in cars, but we had to go in wagons and walk. They would get news on the radio and would tell us when to go. They told us when to travel and when to stop. Sometimes they told us that where we were going there would be no food for the cows and horses, so we were forced to pick up what we could find along the trail. We grabbed wheat bundles and oat bundles and anything else we could find. You couldn't forget your cow and horses. And when we got to a well there would be fighting for a pail of water ... each one wanted to feed his horses and cow right then.

My father Peter died in the Russian village of Arbousenka and was buried in a cherry garden without a casket and wrapped in sheets and blankets. He was buried with a little baby that was born and died that same day. We stopped for half a day for some reason, which I don't know, and we dug a hole and had the burial

----

* There is an interesting 'family' story about the "Trek" picture on the previous page as told by my niece, Mia Nicholson (Suzanne's step-granddaughter). It took place in the 1970's in Berkeley, California after Suzanne had moved there. In Mia's words, "I was perhaps seven or eight and recollect being with Grandma Suzanne one day, when she stopped at a bookstore on Telegraph Avenue and inquired about books on Mennonites and the Ukraine. She left her name and later a woman came to the house with several books. While they were looking through them, Grandma came across this picture on the cover of one of the books and instantly recognized herself and her sister-in-law ... Suzanne walking by a cow and her sister-in-law Mary driving the wagon during the 'trek' out of the Ukraine. Her reaction was poignant! She was obviously moved by the discovery ... almost overcome by the memories it unleashed, sad yet happy, and thanked the visitor warmly, several times." Suzanne's son Arthur has the copy of the book, 'Gedenkbuechlein', Ref. 1.

there. We even had a minister there, an old man. Father was 73 when he died. He died because of the wagon trip. The old people could not stand the cold and there was no warm food.

We slept in barns, oh what I could tell you. In barns full of hay and straw where so many hundreds slept and the straw was crawling with lice. You have no idea how bad it was ... unbelievable, terrible. My little Arthur scratched himself as if he didn't know what was happening to him. I practically had to pick up a stone and kill the lice. Sometimes I wonder how we ever made it. We slept between the cows to keep warm. Can you imagine sleeping between the cows, and in the middle of the night the cow stands up and she lets go! That happened to one woman, she woke up and she had to wipe off her face. Now you know, it sounds funny. Even in this tragedy when we stopped somewhere, someone would start playing an accordion, and we would start singing. Can you imagine that? Beautiful! Then all at once we would have to pack up and hurry on, as again the Russians were coming.

Sometimes during the trek the bandits were after us, and the SS men would gather us together. Some didn't believe in God, but they knew that we did. And Wachman said, "Our God has forsaken us, and you will see that your God has forsaken you." And the other SS man said, "Well women, I have to tell you, we have a very hard trip now. There are bandits on all sides in the timber that we are going through. Pray as you have done, as it is a very dangerous trip." And we went through beautifully!

Once I stole beets in the night from a field and the farmer caught me. I had loaded myself up with beets. He yelled, "What are you doing?" and I said, "I have beets for my cow. We have no milk, if we don't feed her we wont have any milk". And he said, "Don't come any more", and I said, "No". This was a Russian farmer ... there are a lot of good-hearted Russian people. But he said, "Don't come any more", and I said, "I wont". We stole eggs for food when we could find them. Finally, the horses just couldn't go any more. Those poor, beautiful horses ... their feet were bleeding and we had to leave them, but my nephew Henri wanted to die with the horses. He was horse crazy ... he wanted to lie down right there with the horses and die with them. It was very cold. Peter also didn't want to leave the horses, and if Peter's mother, Mary, had not told them they had to leave with us, both Henri and Peter would have stayed there and frozen to death. We had to leave the horses there and go on a train.

Most of the trek was made by wagon, but the last part was by train, because we had to give up the horses. The SS men could have done this a long time before, but they stalled us.

We got to the Polish line just before Christmas in 1943. I said to my sister, "If I can have a corner with straw on the floor and can sleep, that would be the most beautiful Christmas I would ever have." And it happened, even better than I wanted. We were put up in the home of some Russian people, and I got to sleep in a feather bed! They were very nice people ... you couldn't find nicer people. We had church together in the school there. And they made vodka ... very strong vodka, and the little kids drank some vodka too. We were close with them, very close. They told us that if the Germans had just trusted them, they wouldn't have had to fight against them. One Russian girl said to us, "My husband is somewhere in Russia, they took him to work there". And she said, "If you see him (she gave me the address and everything) feed him good and take care of him, and if I see your husband somewhere, I will do the same".

9. Poland

We were there near the Polish border for about three months. Then, all at once in March 1944 there came an order to leave. So this fellow where Arthur and I stayed had to take us to the train station. On the way to the station I met one of the SS men, and he asked if I wanted to catch the train, and I said, "Yes". "Well", he said, "You better ask your man to drive faster, the train is leaving". The man had good horses, but it was slick ice and it was hard for the horses to stay on their feet. They went as fast as they could. We came to the train station and I took Arthur and pushed him onto one of the cars and this Russian fellow, a good fellow, threw my things in. I stepped in as the train was already moving. If we had been just a minute or two minutes later, we wouldn't be here today, we would still be there in Poland, or most likely somewhere back in Russia. It was not a train where you sit down ... it was a train that carried animals ... a cattle train I guess you call it.

We went from the Polish border into Poland* to the city of Mogilno. In Mogilno my sister Sara and I had two rooms. She had a child and I had a child, mine was younger. She got a good job serving in a dining room, and I worked as a barber. This German fellow said to me, "Why don't you go and tell them to give you that barber shop. The Polish fellow that owned it was killed in the war." I could be the boss ... it could have been mine. And I said, "I thank you, I don't want it. I had mine (husband) and he is gone and I don't want what belongs to somebody else". I said, "I will go and work there, but I shall not ask that it be mine". So, I worked there for a while. I think I

---

* About this time Suzanne was separated from part of her family. A 'related' story from her nephew Peter Penner about his mother appears in Chapter 14.

could have been a much better barber ... but I hadn't done it for such a long time. I didn't know how to curl hair, but they were eager to teach me. I did lady's buns by heating the hair with water using tubes. I never had picked that up before, but I practiced and I became pretty good.

It is difficult to say very much about Arthur. You know, a child is a child. They don't care where they go and they are glad to get something to eat. Our (the mothers) main reason for living was so that we could feed the children. We cooked outside and milked the cows outside. The milk was very important for the children. In Poland where we were, Arthur had a sled and went sledding a lot. One day he came back and his head was covered with blood and he was crying hard and I asked what happened. The Polish neighbor boy had beaten him up, because Arthur hadn't given him the sled. I thought it was pretty brave of him to keep the sled even with a bloody nose. He was about 5 then.

We stayed in Mogilno for about ten months ... until January 1945, when again we were forced to leave.

10. 'East' Germany

In January 1945 we had to leave Poland. There were five children in our car, five children and three mothers, and we had just one loaf of bread. It took us three days to get from Poland to eastern Germany. They stopped in the middle of fields where you couldn't get any water, nothing. It was the coldest day in January, and some of the windows were broken. I don't remember the date. My toes were frost-bitten and one baby froze to death in the carriage. And the mother whose baby died was going crazy, going out of her head. When we came to Treuenbrietzen in (east) Germany near Berlin, they put us again in camps. There were babies there whose mothers were either lost or had died. Some mothers may have died, or maybe the babies were put on the train but the mothers were left behind. An elderly couple in Treuenbrietzen that did not have children took home one of the babies, which did not have a mother. The "new father" was so proud that they had a baby and would take it for rides outside in the carriage. He told us the whole room was filled with diapers and he had to tiptoe so not to wake the baby. They didn't know whom it belonged to, but they took it and were so happy.

We were in Treuenbrietzen for about 4 months. This was near Berlin and we could see the American and British planes come, just like a wild goose formation. When they came at night, they would brighten up the sky with flares, like a Christmas tree. Then boom, boom, and again boom, boom. It was one after another. It must have been so bright in Berlin that you could see a needle on the floor. We could easily see the light and we were 50 km from Berlin. Bombs fell near us too, and machine gun shells. We would run to the bunkers. One evening we had the radio on and were told that everyone should leave the city, because it was going to be bombed that night. So we went out and hid in the timber, and stayed there all night. Treuenbrietzen was not bombed, but we had nothing to lose if it was bombed or not. We were with a couple of Germans who wanted to leave and they asked us to go with them to (west) Germany where the Americans and the British were. So we decided to go with them. We started walking and walked from Treuenbrietzen to Kurbolitz, several kilometers away. When we got to Kurbolitz we wanted to cross the river there, but we couldn't, because they had blown up the bridge over the river and we couldn't swim. Some people did swim over. This was the Elbe River. So we stayed there in Kurbolitz. We were there three days and then the Russians said, "How do you do". Well how do you like that ... we had been overrun again, this time by the Russians. They had finally caught up with us. Now I was in the Russian zone. The line agreed to between the Russian zone and the western zone was west of Berlin. German women would hang out white sheets when the Russians came to show they gave up. Lots of German girls hanged themselves before the Russians came, because they were so scared about what they would do to them. We stayed in a schoolroom. There were lots of homeless people like us. The teacher came and said we should occupy two of his rooms because I knew the Russian language. This couple, the teacher and his wife, Mr. and Mrs. Hookal, were very good to us. Arthur was sick then with pneumonia. He was about 6 years old and he started to go to school there with Hookal. Hookal was a very good teacher.

We stayed there for about 6 months, until I was afraid the Russians would send me back to Russia. They had already registered me. I just didn't know what day it would be, but I lived every day in fear. The Russians were sending back to Russia all of their people that the Germans had taken from Russia to work in Germany when the war was on. Lots worked in households and on farms and in factories. Most of them had been sent away already. How they found out that I had lived in Russia, I don't know. I had to go to the office and they registered me too. And so it was for sure that they would send us back to Russia some time. But a very nice friend, who found out that they were about to gather up all these people and send them back, came to me and said I had to leave. His name was Mr. Heabestrite. He had been in an office where he had learned that the Russians had asked all the Germans to let them know where these people were, because they had to go back. And so he told me, and I had to leave. But I didn't know where to go, because to go somewhere on the train you almost always had to have, not exactly a passport but, permission from the mayor so that you could get a train ticket. Otherwise, you couldn't get a train ticket. Then you had to tell the mayor why you were going and where you were going. I couldn't do that, because the mayor was a communist and the German policemen were communists too, so I couldn't say anything. I was so exhausted and so nervous I didn't know what to do or where to go. But Ruth, a girl I knew, told me to go with her to her uncle in Magdeburg, because he knew how to cross to the British side. From Magdeburg I would have to go by train to the British line. It was about 15 kilometers from Kurbolitz to Magdeburg. We walked three miles to the railroad station and asked for three tickets to Magdeburg ... for Ruth, myself and Arthur. And they gave us tickets without asking any questions ... they gave us tickets ... to Magdeburg. We couldn't believe it!

So we made it to Magdeburg and met her uncle. His name was Goldke ... the first name I don't know anymore. Ruth told him my whole story. He had engineer friends who drove the train, and he went right away to the railroad station. He came back in about two hours with tickets for Arthur and me to go to the British line. From there on I was on my own ... how I would get across the line was my problem.

So we went. The train stopped near the line and I was amazed and surprised by such a big camp where already so many Germans wanted to go to the West. But there was a nearby town where I knew a woman. I cannot remember right now what her name was, but her first name was Ella. She had been in Kurbolitz earlier and I had a chance to help her. And I thought, maybe now she could help me. I just knew her street and her name and didn't know anything more. It was snowing. I had this little sled for Arthur, and I put him on the sled with the little bit we had and we walked to that town.

It was snowing and it started to get dark and I didn't know which way to go. One road here, one road there and in between was timber. I was afraid the Russians would catch us, and I stood there and just didn't know where to go. Arthur said, "Mother, do you want to cry?" I said "No, dear," but I cried like a baby. The tears came because I didn't know where to go and night was coming. But I chose the right hand road, and sure enough that was the right one and soon we came to some houses.

I went from door to door and asked people where the street was and if such and such a name lived there. They would tell me a street and we walked and we walked. Then someone would say, you have been walking too far, go back. And then, all at once, we found the number on the fence, and I was sure this was her place. But I was a little worried, so I put Arthur over the fence and Arthur went up and knocked on the door. I heard her say, "Who is there?" He said, "Eeka". She said, "Arthur, is that you, where is your mom?" "Mama is behind the fence." She came and said to me, "Suzanne, do you want to cross the line?" "Oh yes," I said, "but don't say it so loud, someone might hear you." She said, "The line is not too far and maybe the Russian soldiers will let you go through." I said, "Why do you think that?" Well, she said, "You speak the Russian language." I said, "You don't know them. If I go there and talk to them in Russian they would just hold me there and then send me back to Russia. I cannot do that."

But Mr. Goldke had given me addresses of three railroad engineers. These railroads transported coal and other things from east to west and from west to east, and these men would sometimes hide people in the coal cars. So I went to one and he said, "No, I cannot do it." I said, "I have 500 marks, I will give you all my money." He said, "I cannot do it, I'm sorry." So I went to another one and he said the same thing. I went to the third one and he said he could not. He said, "If you had come 10 days earlier, I could have done it. We have done lots of this. But now I cannot do it." And his wife said, "Do you think my husband will give his life for you?" I said, "I don't ask that. I just wanted to see if he could take me over. A friend of yours told me you had done that." Then he told me that he had done it. But the last time the Russian soldiers had blown the whistle for him to stop the train, but he had people hidden in the coal car, so he didn't stop. When he came back, they told him that if he did it once more he would be shot. And that's why the lady said, "Do you think that my husband would give his life for you?"

We had nowhere to go. We had been staying with Ella and her parents for three days now. I didn't sleep, I didn't eat, I thought, "My God, how can I escape?" I would just have given up if I had been alone, but for Arthur I had to go. For myself, I would not have gone a half-mile further.

11. A Way Out!

The third day at Ella's we had dinner together and I was sitting at the table next to her father who was reading a paper. I guess this was a miracle! I just peaked over and I saw this: "Attention! Attention! For all the people from West Germany who live in East Germany and want to go back now to West Germany, tomorrow the 14th of February is the last chance." I said, "Ella could this be for me too?" She said, "Let's try." So right away we walked 4 kilometers to the station and my goodness me, it was full of people and their baggage, all wanting to go to the West. I came to the man in charge and asked if I could go, and he said, "No, it is already filled. Tomorrow you can come." I said, "What kind of papers do I need?" You see, if he saw on my passport that I was born in Russia, they wouldn't let me go and would probably send me back to Russia. He said, "You don't need any passport", and I said, "Nothing?" He said, "Nothing, just maybe 50 pfennigs for each person." I said, "That's all?" And he said, "Yes." I said, "Register me, I will be here tomorrow." So he registered me and I went home that night so happy!! And I could not sleep for happiness ... I could not believe it, maybe it was not true.

The next morning early I got Arthur on the little sled again and off we went. There were two big soldiers with guns at a gate, which we had to go through. Arthur had a Russian cap and I was sure they would recognize him. I didn't breathe, and believe me when I went through I just looked at the snow on the ground, I didn't even look at their faces. I don't know what they looked like, but they were two husky ones. So we went through and we got on the train, which was full. People were sitting on the floor and everywhere, and you know, not one person talked, nobody said a word. Everyone was afraid that maybe someone would come and ask for a passport. Then, after the train started moving, one fellow said, "In twenty minutes we will be in the

British zone." And all at once everybody was talking, just like a bunch of roosters and chickens. Oh my goodness, what a difference. You don't know what a change it was ... like heaven and earth. In the Western Zone the policemen dressed neatly and the busses were ready. They took our children in their arms, put us on a bus and took us to a camp again. We got a straw sack for a bed, a bowl of soup and a little German sausage and bread. That night I had the best sleep in my life. I couldn't believe it ... we were finally over the line !

So, what to do now? You see, I was "black" ... I came over "black". I didn't belong in the West, but I took the chance. The other people were all organized and they had to go further by train. But I went right away and bought a ticket to Bavaria where my sister-in-law lived. This was my sister-in-law Margaret (Abe's wife) and her daughter Zelma. I had written her before and she said the family she lived with, the Forsters, said we could come. The grandmother had passed away and the room was empty, so I could occupy that room. Thank goodness for that.

So I got tickets. But the trains were full, and we had to wait to get both of us on a train. I had to wait because I could not push Arthur through the window and then try to get on, because I could not take the chance of putting him on and then not being able to get on myself. So I had to wait and sure enough, finally a train came that we could both get on together. That was some trip! The railroads and the stations had all been bombed there. We would go for twenty minutes and then sit for three or five hours. All the cars were full 'like herring', and there was only one toilet. But I didn't need to go ... I hadn't eaten for three days. I had a night pot with me for Arthur, and through the window it went! That's the way we traveled. People screamed because they had to go to the bathroom so badly, but they couldn't go, because the bathroom was full. That's the way we traveled to Bavaria. It should have taken maybe 5 hours, but it took three days.

We came to a village, which was 3 kilometers from Niederleierndorf where my sister-in-law lived. You know, I was so nervous. I would have had to wait a couple of hours for the next train to come, which went right behind the yard where Margaret lived. But I could not wait, so I walked. I put Arthur on the sled again and I walked, 3 kilometers, almost 2 miles in the snow, but it was not too cold. It was in the evening. I asked a fellow if that was Niederleierndorf where the lights were and he said yes. So I went towards where the lights were burning and asked some people where the Forsters family lived and they told me where. I knocked on the gate and the door opened. Here I was. My sister-in-law Margaret and I had not seen each other for a long time. We had been separated from each other while in Poland about two years earlier in 1944.

They were pretty surprised to see us, and naturally they wanted to know all that had happened. The reunion was pretty tearful. The Forsters family was very interested to know what the Russians had done in Kurbolitz and those other places where they had lived. They wanted to give me something to eat, and I said, "Give me a piece of bread and milk, that's all I want, we want to go to bed. And I got to sleep in grandma's feather bed, oh boy, oh boy!"

65

12. Refugees Again

The Burgermeister in Niederleierndorf was a friend of the Forsters, so Margaret got a ration card for me. You had to have a ration card or you were lost. They gave Arthur and me ration cards right away, and that was the biggest help I could have, except for being able to stay with the Forsters. There was a building commissar in Regensburg, and he was in charge of all the buildings and houses. He knew exactly how many rooms there were in every house, and how many people they could take in. All the German families had to take people in. There were already three families with the Forsters, and we were the fourth to come. They called me and told me that we had to come to Regensburg to see the commissar.

We got cigarettes in our rations and, since I didn't smoke, I decided to take them to the commissar ... you know, to help convince him. When I got there he said, "Are you Mrs. Stelzig?", and I said, "Yes I am." He said, "You are in Niederleierndorf and you came 'black' over the line." I said, "Yes I did". "Well," he said, "You will have to go back to the Russian zone", and I said, "No, I am not going back". I was holding the cigarettes, but he didn't take any ... he had enough I guess. I thought I could bribe this fellow, but he was a tough one. He said, "You have to go back to the Soviet zone", and I said, "No, I will not go back". And he said, "You people from the east come here just because we live better than the people in eastern Germany". I said, "You are mistaken. I will tell you why I came over. I came over for my boy. For myself, I would not have had the will to come to the West. I don't care for my life. You can shoot me, but I will not go back." He said, "You have to go back".

And I went out and I didn't even cry. Can you believe that, I didn't even cry. But now I was scared ... what shall I do now? My goodness me, I went a couple of streets further and there was an American and Canadian Consul house. I didn't know it was there, but I just walked down the street and there it was ... the Consul. So I went there and knocked on the door and a woman said to come in. I opened the door and I stood and cried, and she said, "What's the matter? Sit down". I said, "Pretty soon I will tell you". After I got myself together, I told her from where I came, that I had come 'black' over the line to West Germany. I told her that all my brothers had been sent to Siberia, that I lost my husband in Leningrad and that my boy would also be sent to Siberia if we were sent back. That was the only reason I came over, for my son. And she asked what I wanted. I told her I wanted to ask the consul if he would give me a paper so that the commissar would leave me alone until I could go to Canada. She was the secretary to the consul and the consul was in Berlin. She said no immigrants could go to Canada then. I said I knew that, but we had learned through a letter that our people in Canada were working with the government there to get us out, and for us to have patience. I told her that I knew there was a boat going to South America in 1947, but that I didn't want to go to South America, to Paraguay ... I wanted to go to Canada. I just wanted the consul to allow us to stay long enough for a chance to go. She said she was sorry, but the consul was not home.

So I left because I didn't get anything there. Then I went to the barracks where some Russians and some of our Mennonite people were. They lived together in the barracks there. I went to them and told them my story. There was a 22 year-old boy there, and he said, "They have no right to send you back. You have a ration card, and if they send you out of Niederleierndorf we have a place with two more beds in the barracks, so you can come here. They cannot send you back to the Soviet zone."

Oh, I was so happy. When you are drowning, you are just grabbing at straws, and with that I went back to the Forsters very happy. I took the train and went home to Niederleierndorf. But I was sitting on needles. The railroad men had on uniforms, and to me they were all policemen. A man with a uniform came along and I ran to the cool room ... where they kept food. I hid there until I knew who he was. I went back to Niederleierndorf and stayed with Margaret and the Forsters and they never bothered me again. My friends said I could come back to the barracks in Regensburg, if I was bothered again. But the officials never bothered me again.

Arthur at age 8 when he and Suzanne were living in Niederleierndorf.

While we were in Germany for that year and a half or two, I lived with and worked for the Forsters in Bavarian. We did their housework and even helped in the field. They didn't want me in the field too much ... Margaret was good in the field, but I was not so good. We sewed for them, we spun wool for them and we knit for them, did crochet work for them, and things like that. They would give us bread and some milk. Margaret would milk the cows and every day would get a liter of milk. And that was very good. The Forsters were very quiet and didn't trust us right away. They killed pigs, but were not allowed to kill more pigs than the burgermeister allowed, because most of the pigs should go for meat for other people. One day Zelma, Margaret's little girl, was in the barn for potatoes and she saw a big pig hanging there. She came and she said, "Mama, they have killed a pig." The Forsters were so scared that we would go tell the burgermeister that they had killed a pig when they shouldn't. I could see that Mrs. Forster's face was red and her eyes were flashing. She was so nervous and I said, "Mrs. Forster, don't be afraid of us, we will never tell them. You work hard and it's yours. We would never tell that you killed a pig." My goodness, we got meat then. Each time they killed a pig they gave us meat and lard.

We got along very well together. They took in four families ... four people from Czechoslovakia and six from Russia, ten people altogether. And we cooked on one stove. I don't think I would have been as good as the Forsters were. They were so good!

Probably the barracks in West Germany where Arthur says they lived briefly while their deportation papers were being processed.

69

Then came the time that the Durksen's* wrote from Pincher Creek, in Canada. The relatives of the people in Canada could come over, but I didn't know where my relatives were in Canada. My father's cousins were somewhere in Canada, but I had no idea where. Margaret called Mr. and Mrs. Durksen her uncle and aunt, but they were not blood relations. The Durksen's asked the Canadian government to get their niece over, and they allowed Margaret and Zelma to come. Mr. Durksen was my brother Isaac's friend in Russia, and they knew us very well. So they asked if I would like to come, if they could arrange it. But he said, "You have to believe like Abraham did when he had to offer his son." I wrote the next day: "I'm coming, I'm ready, I don't care where I go, I just want out." You know, they had no trouble getting me into Canada. They said they didn't know how it happened. He went to Ottawa and got permission for us to come.

We went to the doctor for a checkup first, and then to the consul. They really questioned us. They didn't want Communists going to Canada. They didn't know what kind of people we were, maybe Communists. He asked where I had worked in Russia, what I had done in Russia, where I was born, what I would do in Canada and how I knew this family in Canada. I said I knew them since I was a little girl, and told him I would work on their farm. That's what I told them, but I had no idea what I would do. I didn't think I would do that, but I say funny things sometimes! But I said I would work on their farm, so that maybe he would let us get through. So he filled out some forms. We

----

* Suzanne had a document in her various papers, which was an 'Affirmation of David Durksen' written in Pincher Creek on March 1, 1947. The 'Affirmation' (to the Canadian governmnet) supports Suzanne coming to Canada and pledges to pay all costs of her and Arthur's travel to Alberta and guarantees that he will support her once in Alberta, so that she will not become a 'public charge.

70

then went to another room, where there was a secretary and another fellow, and my goodness, they gave us passports! When he stamped it, Arthur said to me, "Mother is that what we want?" And I said, "That is it!" and the consul said, "I'll see you in Canada." Arthur and I were speaking German and he asked the secretary what we said and she told him we were just very happy.! So we got our passports and not long afterward we left for Canada in October 1948.

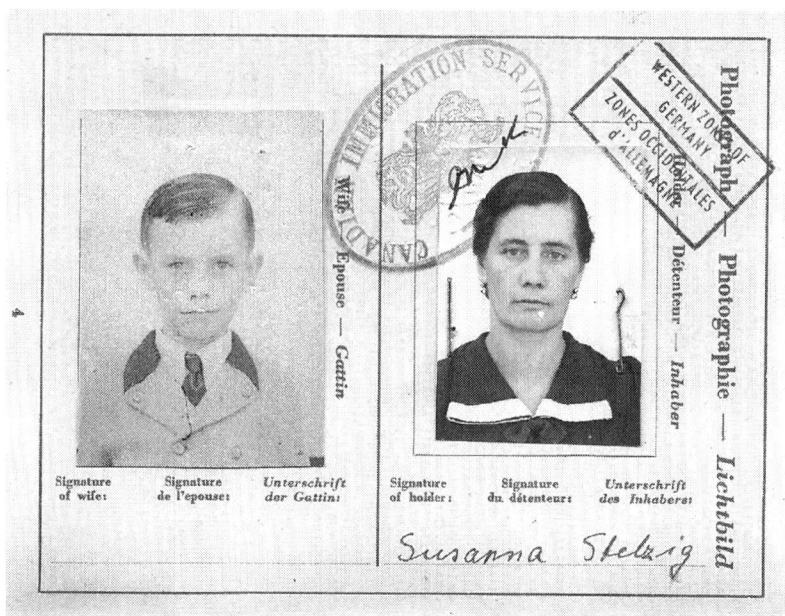

The above is the fourth page from the 'Temporary Travel Document' which was to Suzanne and Arthur for travel to Canada.

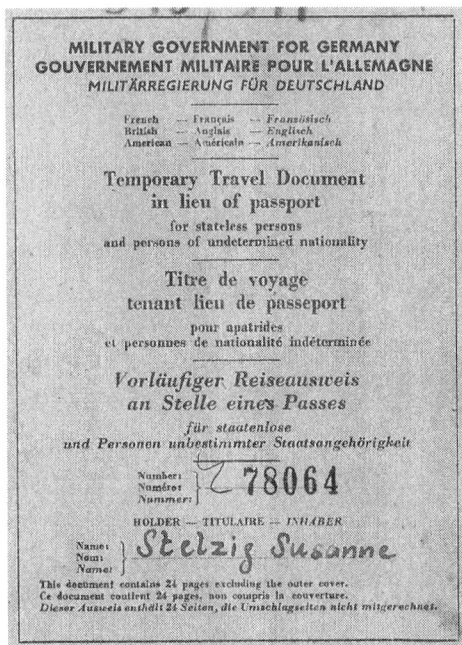

MILITARY GOVERNMENT FOR GERMANY
GOUVERNEMENT MILITAIRE POUR L'ALLEMAGNE
MILITÄRREGIERUNG FÜR DEUTSCHLAND

French — Français — *Französisch*
British — Anglais — *Englisch*
American — Américain — *Amerikanisch*

Temporary Travel Document
in lieu of passport
for stateless persons
and persons of undetermined nationality

Titre de voyage
tenant lieu de passeport
pour apatrides
et personnes de nationalité indéterminée

*Vorläufiger Reiseausweis
an Stelle eines Passes*
*für staatenlose
und Personen unbestimmter Staatsangehörigkeit*

Number:
Numéro: 78064
Nummer:

HOLDER — TITULAIRE — *INHABER*

Name:
Nom: Stelzig Susanne
Name:

This document contains 24 pages excluding the outer cover.
Ce document contient 24 pages, non compris la couverture.
Dieser Ausweis enthält 24 Seiten, die Umschlagseiten nicht mitgerechnet.

Above is the front page of the 'Temporary Travel Document' issued to Suzanne and Arthur. Note that it was issued by the 'Military Government for Germany' and was for stateless persons and persons of undetermined nationality, in lieu of a passport.

72

This is likely the train Suzanne and Arthur took from where they had been staying in Niederleierndorf to where they embarked for Canada.

Suzanne and Arthur on the train prior to their embarkation to Canada. This is likely the same train as the 'train' photo above.

73

13. Canada and Beyond

We left for Canada by ship in October 1948.* The ship was the *Marina Tiger* and it was a beautiful ship! We didn't have money, but the Canadian government gave us some money for travel. But I was sick much of the trip. The passengers ate in two groups in the dining hall and we were in the second group. We had to wait until the first group was finished, and by that time I was seasick and couldn't eat. And the people said how good it was. The grapefruit ... I had never seen one ... they looked so

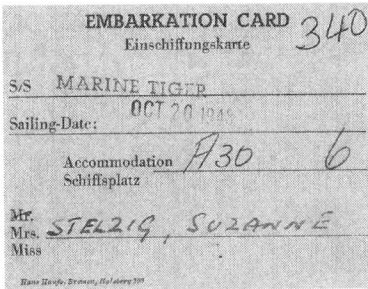

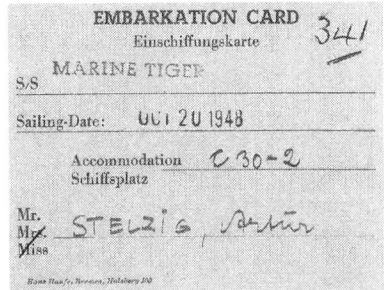

These are Embarkation Cards issued to Suzanne and Arthur for sailing on the Marine Tiger, dated October 20, 1948.

----

* Arthur says they left from Bremerhaven. According to the Port of Halifax Pier 21 website (www.pier21.ca/home) the Marine Tiger arrived at Halifax on October 29, 1948 with 600 passengers for Canada. The ship was one of a class of C4 troop ships built by Kaiser Shipyard, Vancouver, Wash. She was completed in July 1945 and could accommodate 3,800 troops, but was later converted to a passenger ship. On June 24th 1947 she began her first trans-Atlantic voyage under charter to United States Lines, with accommodation for 850 tourist class passengers. Her last voyage on this service was in September 1949.

good, but I couldn't eat. I was so sick! I met a nice friend, who had been a doctor in Russia and had made it to Germany and was now going to Canada. Her name was Catherine Koch. She said to me, "Suzanne, you have to get up and have some grapefruit." She got me up and I went just like a drunken one to the table ... it was terrible. Catherine was so anxious to get cigarettes so she could smoke, but she had lost her taste for cigarettes due to seasickness. But Arthur was just as alive as could be ... he never stayed in bed. And Arthur, did he ever like Coca Cola! It was first time he had tasted it. Arthur was happy all the time, but I was not. For those who didn't get sick it was a wonderful trip.

The "Marina Tiger" (Marine Tiger) took Suzanne and Arthur from Bremerhaven to Halifax, Canada. It arrived at Halifax on October 29, 1948 and Suzanne and Arthur were processed the next day.

We arrived in Halifax near the end of October ... I don't recall the exact date*. We all had numbers indicating where we

----

* It was October 29 and they were processed the next day on October 30, 1948.

75

Above are the 'Immigration Identification Cards' issued to Suzanne and Arthur on their arrival in Halifax, dated October 30, 1948.

were to go. For us it was Pincher Creek, Alberta, so from Halifax we had to travel almost all the way across Canada by train. What surprised me most about Canada was seeing a little house with a car beside it. I expected a large expensive house, if there was a car !

A picture of immigrants waiting to board the train in Halifax for trips to their final destination ... some as far west as Alberta where Suzanne and Arthur were destined. This may or may not be Suzanne and Arthur's group, but it is a group of immigrating Mennonites. Note the boxes and bales, and the scarcity of suitcases. The sign on the train reads "Luggage Room".

Before we got to Pincher Creek, we stopped in Lethbridge, Alberta. We stopped right in front of a park for maybe an hour and I got off the train. They were raking the fall leaves and I said to myself, if I come to a town like this I will like it ... that park was so beautiful. But we had to go further and then we came to Pincher Station, and there were hardly any houses ... no town and there was snow on the ground. (I didn't know then that the town was 2 miles from the station.) Oh, I felt so sorry for the poor cows, which were out in the snow. Mr. and Mrs. Durksen met us at the station. We hadn't seen them for years and years. They took us to Pincher Creek where their son Pete worked at Morgan's garage. He looked us over, probably thinking, "Here were some wild ones coming now". He and his family were going to the farm that day, so we left with them for the farm that evening.

Suzanne and Arthur at Durksen farm and Suzanne feeding the turkeys.

My goodness, I thought I would never see a town again. The farm was seven miles from town, and I couldn't walk that far and I couldn't drive the car. When we got to the Durksens farm Irma had the table set, oh so beautiful! There was white bread and black bread and homemade butter and cheese. It was something out of this world. They gave us a nice room upstairs, and the next morning I looked out the window and the beautiful cows and other cattle were lying down and they were covered with snow, and I said to myself, it's hard to be a cow in Canada. And when I wrote to my friends in Germany, I told them one thing, "I wouldn't want to be a cow in Canada". In Germany and Russia we kept our farm animals in barns.

I was with the Durksens for about two weeks. There was a German farmer who wanted me to help his family before I came over. They knew the Durksens would get a woman. I told the

A picture of the Mennonite Brethren Church congregation near the Durksen farm. Mr. Durksen is on the far right, Suzanne is in the middle of the group and Arthur is in the front row.

78

Durksons I didn't want to live with Germans, because I wouldn't learn the English language there. I wanted to go to English people and learn to speak English. So a chance came to work for some French-Canadian people, the Pelletiers. Old Mr. Pelletier came to see me, and I understood him when he came. He told me about his wife and what I would do. The Pelletiers had a big house in town and she had boarders. She liked to make money, and did she make money! She paid me $40 a month, but I had to really work hard for it.

Mrs. Pelletier didn't want Arthur to stay at her place. Arthur had to stay with the Durksens at the farm, and he could come just once each week to see me. Mrs. Pelletier was stingy. When she and her husband went to Florida for one winter, she said I could have Arthur stay with me. But she said I would have to buy the milk for him. I bought for him a liter of milk every day.

There were four men who lived with the Pelletiers: their son George Pelletier, Dr. Gerry Nicholson, Norman Bode and Lloyd Christianson. And in the wintertime, an older lady, Mrs. Hyde, was there quite a bit. I worked hard at the Pelletiers. Mrs. Pelletier had a big garden and grew a lot of their vegetables. I did the cooking and washing for all those people. We had to hang the wash outside to dry, and sometimes Mr. Pelletier's underwear would be blown into the neighbors garden, frozen stiff and standing up there. And the sheets would be frozen and cracked.

Dr. Nicholson was a young doctor, and the hospital was just across from the Pelletiers. I did his laundry and he paid me well. He was a fine fellow and I said to Mrs. Pelletier, "He must be good, he has a bible in his room". Gerry had a girlfriend, and one time he said to Mrs. Pelletier, "I will not be home for supper, I will have supper with my girlfriend." I said to Mrs. Pelletier, "Who is his girlfriend?" I didn't speak very good English ... I don't even speak good English now, but worse then. She said, "She works at Cornyn's Drugstore." The next day I went to the drugstore to look over that girl. Dr. Nicholson was such a nice fellow, and I wanted to see this girlfriend of his. I don't know what I bought there, but I bought something and I looked her over. She had red hair and was nicely dressed. She looked real nice and she was very friendly. So then I knew who she was, but I didn't know her parents.

Then Gerry and Shirley got married and Gerry invited me to the wedding. After they were married, Gerry and Shirley took an apartment at the Pelletiers, so we saw each other practically every day. And we became friends. Then they moved to California where he worked at a hospital in San Francisco. Shirley sent a present for me, and her brother Gary brought it to me. At that time I happened to be at Mrs. Hyde's. I didn't know him then, but here comes Gary so polite with a present from his sister. I liked that boy right away.

I was at the Pelletiers for almost four years, until the fall of 1952. I left the Pelletiers because I had to work so hard there. Mrs. Pelletier was really a good honest woman. She could not help it, but she liked to work and she liked to see me work too. The doctor told me I had swollen muscles in my neck from working so hard. I also had been painting the house outside. He said I would have to stop that, and told me just to tell Mrs. Pelletier that I had to have two or three weeks holiday. So I told her and she was sorry. Then she decided herself that she would let me go, and I was so pleased that I didn't need to tell her that I wanted to leave.

About then Mrs. Hyde, who had often visited Mrs. Pelletier, became sick. Her daughter, Irene, came from Montreal and when she heard that I wouldn't be going back to the Pelletiers, she came right away and asked me to stay with her mother and that's what I did. With Mrs. Hyde it was a much easier life. I had Arthur with me, and that was the first real home we had in a long time. But Mrs. Hyde was elderly and quite sick and she died the next spring (1953).

After Mrs. Hyde passed away, I went with Arthur to take care of Mr. and Mrs. Staunton*. I stayed with the Stauntons for about four years. They were the nicest people you ever could meet. They were a lady and a gentleman and down-to-earth. They adopted Arthur just like their own child. I never had seen people like that. She lived to be 102 years old. Mr. Staunton was not a very good driver. There were so many bumps in his car, but he always said it was the fault of the other fellow. Whether it was $50, $60 or $80, it was never his fault, always somebody else's fault. They wanted me to drive their car and they thought I could learn to drive ... just like that. They had so much faith in me, and it scared me to pieces. Several times I had to drive them to their ranch outside of Pincher Creek, and I really didn't know how to drive very well. I must have had a guardian angel, as I didn't dump them all in the ditch, but one time it was very close. I had just started driving and they thought I knew everything already, but I didn't. Mr. Staunton thought he was a pretty good driver, but she thought I was better than Dick, her husband. One time coming home from their son Frank's ranch he went right into the ditch with Mrs. Staunton and the kids ... went slowly in, but didn't hit or hurt anybody.

The Vliets had bought Mrs. Hyde's house after she passed away and I was very close to that house, because that was where Arthur and I really had good times with Mrs. Hyde. She had treated him so well, and it was just like a home to me. While we were at the Stauntons, Mrs. Vliet became very sick. Irma Durksen took care of Mrs. Vliet for a while, and since I had some afternoons off I would also go there and help. Sometimes I

---

*   It was while Suzanne and Arthur were at the Stauntons that Arthur recalls her receiving a Red Cross message informing her that her husband Gena has died during the Leningrad siege. It is interesting that she did not mention this during the telling of her story, but Arthur recalls it well. See p. 93.

Suzanne and Arthur, and Suzanne ... in the back yard of the Vliet house (the old Hyde house) in Pincher Creek. These may have been taken during the time Suzanne was helping take care of Mrs. Vliet.

would go to the Vliet house and the dishes were all in the sink. I would wash them and put them away and go to the store. I had to get away from the Stauntons once in a while. Even though they were very good to us, I couldn't stay in that house all the time.

Mrs. Vliet passed away in late spring 1955 and Shirley had come from California to help out. Shirley asked me if I would come and work for her dad and Leslie. I said I could not leave the old folks, as they needed me. But I told her that Mrs. Staunton let me go every afternoon and that I would do what I could do in the house. And that's what I did. Every Friday I would go shop for some fish, make a white sauce, put it in the oven and put a note on the table, telling them what was in the oven. If they could read it I don't know. I would do the washing and the ironing. I also worked part time for the Red Cross in Pincher Creek.

But after two years, in November 1957, Mr. Vliet (Clark) and I got married **. Later I said to Gerry, Dr. Nicholson, "You put us in this mixture. It was your doing." Arthur and Leslie finished high school in Pincher Creek and we came down to live in Berkeley where Clark had bought a house earlier. The boys first went to City College in Oakland, and later to the University of California in Berkeley.

Arthur completed his Mechanical Engineering degree at University of California (Berkeley) in 1962 and got a job with DuPont in Brockville, Ontario in Canada. About a year later he met a very nice girl, Evelyn Leggett, and on the 10th of July 1965 Arthur and Evelyn were married. Evelyn's mother had passed away many years before. Evelyn's father Charles was 82 and he lived with his son Carl and his family in the big old family house on the family farm in Crosby, about forty miles from Brockville. The Leggetts have a lot of cows and sell milk. They also make maple syrup from the maple trees in their "sugar bush". Mr. Leggett showed us their sugar bush while we were there ... very interesting that "sugar bush". Leslie, Gary, Donna and I attended the wedding, and it was very special for me ... my only son, who had escaped from Russia with me, was getting married!

** When Susanne and Clark decided to marry, Suzanne was still legally married to Gena Stelzig. A document from the Supreme Court of Alberta found in Suzanne's various papers states that Suzanne had submitted a petition to the court on April 11, 1957. The court document (May 6, 1957) decreed that, "George Augustus Steliz, husband of said Suzanne Stelzig, is presumed to be dead". The petition Suzanne submitted was not among her papers, so what specifically it contained is unknown. Presumably it explained that she last saw her husband Gena Stelzig in Leningrad in June 1941 and that his last contact with her was from Leningrad a few weeks later. Whether it refers to the Red Cross letter stating that Gena did in fact die in Leningrad during the siege, as Arthur says, is unknown. In any case, Suzanne and Clark Vliet were married in Pincher Creek, Alberta on November 23, 1957.

Suzanne and Arthur in Berkeley sometime during his time at the University of California, Berkeley.

A typical 'Suzanne' dinner at the Vliet house at 2623 College Avenue in Berkeley. Clockwise: Gerry and Shirley Nicholson, Suzanne, Arthur, Gary and Clark, with Les probably taking the picture. The fare is most likely roast beef, mashed potatoes and green peas, and the dessert very possibly Suzanne's 'famous' German chocolate cake.

Arthur and Evelyn were married in the local church, which is just a short walk from the Leggett's farm … you can see the church from the Leggett house. Evelyn's father started the church many years before and still took care of it. Gary was an usher. Leslie was best man and made a toast at the wedding, and that speech I cannot say, but it was beautiful. Whatever Leslie does, it has a good taste!

Suzanne's hope was a good future for Arthur. Here part of that hope comes true. Left: Suzanne and Arthur, and Right: Arthur and Evelyn at their wedding, July 10, 1965

And now Arthur and Evelyn have two wonderful children … Patti and Jimmy … my grandchildren! My boy Arthur is married and has two children ... that's really the life that I wanted for my boy ... that's why I brought him over!

Another hope of Suzanne's comes true. Suzanne reads
to her grandchildren Jimmy and Patti in Berkeley.

Clark and Suzanne on visit to Austin Texas in 1973.

Suzanne had been diagnosed with cancer in 1973, and after treatment she lived for five more years. During her last couple years, she was burdened by Mr. Vliet's worsening condition of senility (Alzheimer's ?). On June 2, 1978 she passed away in Oakland. Suzanne's funeral service was held at the First Presbyterian Church in Berkeley, where she had been very much involved with a women's group, particularly its women's sewing group. Suzanne was interred at the Mountain View Cemetery in Oakland, on a hillside overlooking the Bay toward San Francisco.

Suzanne's gravestone at the Mountain View Cemetery in Oakland, California.

14. A Related Story*

Suzanne's Sister-in-Law is allowed to come to the West.

Sometime, while in Poland in early 1944, Suzanne and Arthur were separated from other members of the family, namely Peter and Walter Penner and their mother Maria. Shortly thereafter, Peter (then about 17) and Walter were conscripted into the German army. On New Year's Eve 1944 Peter arrived at the western front near the border with France, but with little training and poor equipment. He had a number of close-call experiences in those few months near the end of the war, when he could have been killed, but miraculously survived. Finally, he was captured by American forces and briefly was a prisoner of war. He was not aware at the time what had happened to his mother.

A few years after being released, he began a career with a German electrical company and lived in Heilbronn in south Germany. In the interim, Peter's brother Walter immigrated to Paraguay and while there met some people who had relatives in Siberia. Walter sent a letter to them inquiring where his mother Maria might be. She had been separated from her sons and other family members while in Poland in 1944. After this request traveled to several persons in Siberia, it finally reached Maria who was 2000 km away from the people Walter first contacted! Maria had been discovered by the Russians in Berlin shortly after the end of the war and had been shipped to Siberia, even though she was originally from the Ukraine.

In the summer of 1965 it was announced in Germany that Alexander Adjubej, President Nikita Khrushchev's son-in-law and then manager of a large Soviet Government newspaper,

---

* This story is taken from a draft of Peter Penner's memoire. (Peter was Suzanne's nephew and passed away in 2012.)

would be visiting West Germany. Adjubej had been publicly critical of conditions in West Germany, so three West German newspapers had invited him to come and see "how bad" conditions 'really' were in West Germany. His first day was to be in the industrial town of Dortmund, where he would stay at the Four Seasons Hotel. Peter saw this as a great opportunity to approach him and plead for his mother's release. He took the week off from work and the day before this important foreign visit he and his wife drove to Dortmund in their little VW Beatle. In the hotel lobby he heard that Adjubej would be taking a walking trip of downtown Dortmund, so he and Erica followed him and his escort. When Adjubej temporarily left his escort to enter a cigarette store, Peter saw his opportunity. As Adjubej came out, Peter approached him and said in Russian, "Good morning mister Adjubej" and Adjubej thought Peter was Russian. Peter said, "No I am German, but was born in Russia and the reason for talking to you is my mother. She is also German, but was taken by Russian soldiers from Berlin and shipped to Siberia 20 years ago and I am asking you, why your government does not let a 65 year old lady go to live with her two sons in Germany?" Peter asked a few more questions, and gave Adjubej a copy of a letter he'd written which included important information on his mother and himself. Adjubej said, "Mr. Penner your mother will be released in three months", and they shook hands. After walking a short distance from Peter, he returned and said, "Mr. Penner, I promise you your mother will be with you in one month!" Peter was overjoyed and he and Erica spent a couple days at a lake resort on their way home.

Then, just a week later Peter learned that Khrushchev had been removed from power. This meant that Adjubej had likely been replaced, so most likely he would not have issued the necessary order. Peter was devastated, and assumed that his chance to get his mother out of the Soviet Union had vanished. However, about a month later he heard from his mother that something unusual was going on. She had been called into the local police office in Siberia and for the first time in 20 years the police had been polite to her and called her Mrs. Penner, while previously referring to her as "old baba" (old wife). She was asked to provide information on her past and where her sons were living. Peter saw this as good news. Three months later, Peter's mother was given an exit visa and arrived by train in West Germany. Apparently Adjubej was true to his word and must have submitted the order immediately, as he would not have had the authority to do so after he was replaced. Maria's coming to West Germany was widely reported in the West German press. She stayed with Peter in Heilbronn and told of her 20 years confinement in Siberia. She worked in a factory as a metalworker, and was paid but not very much. She lived in a 12 x 16 foot hut, and planted some vegetables for food to supplement what she could buy with the little money from her factory job.

In 1966 Peter's mother was able to travel to Canada to visit her other son Walter. Walter had left Paraguay after being there for several years and, after spending a few years in Germany, had settled in Kitchener, Ontario. Within two months of arriving in Canada, Maria suffered a heart attack and passed away.

After Peter retired, in 1979, he immigrated to Canada and first settled in Apsley, Ontario, and then moved to L'Amble, Ontario. Peter passed away in 2012

15. Her Son's Recollections

I (Arthur) have no recollection of my father or Leningrad, since I was about two when my mom and I left Leningrad and went to the Ukraine to visit with relatives. And I have little recollection of the village where we stayed in the Ukraine, as we were there for only about two years before we were forced to leave on the trek west.

My earliest recollection was when I was four in the fall of 1943 on the wagon train pulled by horses and oxen, heading west to Poland. Most of my memories are a blur. Mud and snow and being cold seem to stick in my mind, along with bumping along in the wagon across the roads of sorts or trails through fields. Heading into heavily wooded or forested areas and being made aware of having to be quiet when 'partisans' or 'bandits' were known to be in the area. No sense of hardship - not even hunger, although there must have been lots of that. It was probably more of an adventure for me as my mom was always there for me. I don't recall any real sense of danger. I do hazily recall staying in a village in Poland, and breaking some windows in a barn and causing a lot of problems for mom. Another was having a sled and going sledding, and hanging on to 'my' sled for dear life when some kids tried to take it away from me. And getting whacked across the nose a few times (and bleeding profusely) and running back to 'mom' crying a river, but hanging on to that darn sled. Again no sense of deprivation, as I was perhaps in my own little world. Also Mom doing some hair cutting for people.

In eastern Germany I do recollect the ongoing bombing, the air raid sirens, our running to the air raid shelters and the vibrations from the bombing. I recall collecting foil strips dropped by planes. I think the foil strips were dropped to confuse radar prior to bombing raids. I think mom scolded me for running to collect the foil strips, as she feared that stuff might

91

explode. I seemed to have known the sirens meant to run to the shelters and to be able to leave when the all-clear siren sounded. I did a lot of walking and hanging on to my mom's hand, and mom was always trying to find food. When the Russians overran the area, I recall my mom's anxiety. I don't think I knew why, but did know mom was trying to get away. Mom talked with some of the Russian soldiers, in particular one officer who seemed to be in charge of the local area who seemed to like me. Mom always had me with her. She said the Russians really liked children, so maybe I served some purpose. Mom taught me an old Russian children's poem, which I recited (in Russian) to the army officer. He liked it so much he gave me some chocolate (I later realized I liked the Cadbury bars from American GI's a whole lot better, since the Russian chocolate didn't seem to be sweet ... kind of bitter, but at the time it was great stuff). I think mom sometimes acted as an interpreter for the Russians when dealing with Germans, and therefore they didn't send her (and me) back to the Siberian paradise, as quickly as they might have otherwise. I vaguely recall going to some kind of school taught by someone that mom seemed to know. Also, some recollection of a train station, people milling around, the train ride across the line, and me sticking my head out the train window and getting some soot particles in my eyes.

I do have recollection of living with the Forsters in Bavaria (Niederleierndorf) and going to school there, but the details are very fuzzy. Mom doing a lot of spinning (wool) on a wooden spinning machine, going to live in some barracks for a while where other refugees were temporarily housed (prior to going on the boat I think), kicking a soccer ball around with a bunch of kids, and chocolate bars tossed to us kids by GI's.

The boat ride across the Atlantic was great fun for me, but mom was sick most of the time. We had food and lots of goodies ... chocolate bars and Coca Cola all the time. There was stormy weather part of the time that caused plates of food to crash to the floor. I recall landing at Halifax and getting on a train, and the seemingly never-ending train ride across Canada. Lots of food and being rocked to sleep in the berths and the hooting of the train whistle.

I think Mom thought we'd never get to 'Pincher Creek'. At Pincher Station the Durksens were waiting for us and we were taken to the farm. Mom couldn't get over the availability of food at the Durksens. In particular, she was fascinated by 'white bread' and remarked on it several times. For me it was the corn flakes.

Mom got a job looking after the Pelletier household and their boarders. She always looked forward to my once a week stay with her there and so did I. Her favorite boarder there by far was Dr. Gerry Nicholson. I think she thought he walked on water. She worked extremely hard at the Pelletiers and was constantly on her feet, and this eventually gave her health problems. Still, she seemed to be always cheerful and didn't complain. The health problems ultimately caused her to leave the Pelletier household, and she began looking after Mrs. Hyde, an elderly lady who lived near downtown on main-street. Later she took care of Mr. and Mrs. Staunton who lived in a nice house in town but further west. She was particularly happy that I could stay with her when she looked after Mrs. Hyde and the Stauntons, and so was I.

While at the Stauntons, I clearly remember one particular morning she was at the kitchen table reading a letter she had just received, which had come from the Red Cross. The letter confirmed that my father had indeed died in 1943 in Leningrad. She had long suspected this to be the case. She was sad and upset for a considerable period of time after that. I think she didn't want to show too much grief, because it might upset me too much. Since I was too young to remember my father, I didn't seem to have the same level of grief, but at least she knew of his fate for certain.

Les Vliet and I had become really good friends and I dropped by the 'Vliet' store almost every day on my way from school to have friendly chats/discussions/arguments with Les's dad (I called him Mr. Vliet) about various events of the day or week or year. I really liked Les's dad and always looked forward to stopping by the 'store'. After Les's mom passed away, my mom would fairly frequently stop by their house to help out and sometimes prepare meals for Les and his dad.

After a period of time I knew that Mom and Les's dad were attracted to each other, and Mom talked with me about them possibly getting married. Les's dad also talked with me about getting married to my mom. I told him that not only did I not have any objections, I was very happy about the situation and thought that Mom would be much happier as well. She had worked so hard all her life and deserved more happiness. And we instantly inherited a family and I now had two brothers and a sister.

While in Berkeley with Gerry and Shirley Nicholson, Mom really became attached to the Nicholson kids. I had already moved to Brockville, but could tell she doted on those 'kids'. After Evelyn and I got married and Patti and Jimmy arrived, Mom was so very happy to have grandchildren. She doted on them whenever we came to visit, and she wished we were closer together. Jimmy and Patti always remember their time with 'Grandma'. They still talk about making cookies with Grandma at the kitchen table … helping to roll the dough and then using a glass to form the cookies, with Patti ever so careful to get exactly the right shape and Jim just going bang, bang, bang with the glass!

I will always remember Mom for her kindness and her selflessness and so often putting the needs of others before her own. Her courage and perseverance, in overcoming what seemed to be almost insurmountable odds in order to get her son to a place with a better life and future, amazes me to this day.

Art Stelzig, April 2010

94

16. Suzanne's Timeline

Mar. 18, 1909 – Suzanne Penner is born in Konteniusfeld.

1917 - The Revolution begins.

1921 - Communists take over.

Sept. 3, 1928 - Suzanne's mother Marie dies of dropsy.

1929 or 1930 - Sisters Katherine and Mary get married and move to the far-eastern Soviet Union near China on the Amur River.

1930 - Brother Isaac leaves collective for Makeyevka.

Dec. 1930 - The village of Konteniusfeld is collectivized.

Jan. 1931 - Suzanne, Sara and Abraham leave for Makeyevka, where Isaac has been working, and spend almost 3 years there.

Summer 1933 - Suzanne and Sara go to Caucasus to work briefly at an agricultural research laboratory run by a German woman.

Autumn 1933 - Suzanne and Sara return to Konteniusfeld and work on the collective.

1934 - Suzanne and Sara invited to work in Leningrad. Sara has married and stays in Konteniusfeld, but Suzanne leaves for Leningrad.

October 28, 1935 - Suzanne marries Gena Stelzig in Leningrad.

1936 - Suzanne's father-in-law, Theodore Stelzig, dies in Leningrad. Suzanne's brother-in-law Arthur Stelzig disappears ... most likely taken by the NKVD.

1937 or 1938 - Suzanne's brothers Isaac, Peter and Abraham are taken away while Suzanne is in Leningrad.

June 20, 1939 - Arthur is born in Leningrad.

June 19, 1941 - Suzanne and Arthur leave Leningrad for Konteniusfeld to visit her family, with Gena expecting to join them in a few weeks.

June 22, 1941 - Suzanne and Arthur arrive in Konteniusfeld, and find Germany began their invasion of the Soviet Union during their trip. In the following few weeks she receives three telegrams and some money from Gena, then no further word from him.

Early Fall 1941 – Before the German army overruns their area, the Communists attempt to ship Suzanne and Arthur and thousands of other Mennonites east beyond the Urals, but the plan is foiled. They return to their pillaged village.

Late October 1941 – Konteniusfeld is overrun by the German army during its advance toward Stalingrad.

August 1942 – February 1943 – Battle of Stalingrad takes place and German armies capitulate and begin retreat in February.

Oct. 1943 – German army nears Konteniusfeld during retreat from Stalingrad, and the "trek" westward for Suzanne and Arthur and thousands of other Mennonites begins by foot and wagon.

Dec. 1943 - During 'trek' Suzanne's father Peter dies and is buried in an orchard in the small Russian village of Arbousenka.

Near Christmas 1943 - "Trek" ends near the Polish border. For 3 months Suzanne and Arthur live in temporary quarters.

March 1944 – Because of the advance of the Russian army, Suzanne and Arthur take train into Poland to Mogilno, and spend about 10 months there. It is during this hectic train trip that Suzanne and Arthur are separated from much of the family.

Jan. 1945 - As front advances, again they are forced to take train into Germany (eastern Germany) to Treunbrietzen near Berlin. They spend 4 months there until a few days before the war ends.

Early May 1945 - Suzanne and Arthur walk to Kurbolitz (about 15 km) and a few days later on May 6th the war ends, leaving them in the Russian zone! They are there about 9 months, until fear of being shipped back to the Soviet Union causes them to leave.

Feb. 1946 - Suzanne and Arthur are able to escape to West Germany, where they live as refugees in Niederleierndorf (near Regensburg) for two-and-a-half years.

Oct. 1948 - Suzanne and Arthur leave West Germany by ship for Canada, and arrive at Halifax on October 29. They are processed on Oct. 30 and then travel by train to Pincher Creek, Alberta.

1948 – 1957 - Suzanne first works for Mrs. Pelletier and later takes care of Mrs. Hyde and then Mr. and Mrs. Staunton.

Nov. 1957 - Suzanne and Clark Vliet marry in Pincher Creek and with Arthur and Leslie move to Berkeley, California.

Jan 1963 - Arthur graduates in Mechanical Engineering from the University of California, Berkeley and takes a position with DuPont in Brockville, Ontario.

July 10, 1965 - Arthur marries Evelyn Leggett in the Leggett family church in Crosby, Ontario, and Suzanne attends. With her escape to West Germany, her immigration to Canada, Arthur's graduation from UC Berkeley and now Arthur's marriage, most of Suzanne's hopes are fulfilled.

June 2, 1978 - Suzanne passes away in Oakland, California and is buried in Oakland's Mountain View Cemetery.

17. Suzanne's Family as Related by Suzanne

The Penners:

<u>Grandmother</u>: Gertrude (Koop) Penner. (Her only son Peter was Suzanne's father), (Gertrude died at 77 in 1932 or '33)

<u>Father</u>: Peter (died at 73 during "trek" out of Russia in late fall of 1943 and was buried in a cherry orchard in the small Russian village of Arbousenka.)

<u>Mother</u>: Marie (Franzen), (died Konteniusfeld Sept. 3, 1928)

<u>Children</u>:

<u>Isaac</u>: m. Maria Wiens (Hans, Maria, Peter and Walter), (last seen 1937-38, taken away by local police or NKVD)

<u>Peter</u>: m. Suzanne Kliewer (Suzanne, Mary, Peter, Gertrude, Elizabeth, Hilda and Henry), (last seen 1937-38, taken away by local police or NKVD)

<u>Elizabeth</u>: m. Henry Kasper (Henry, Elizabeth and Maria), (sent to city of New Siberia after war)

<u>Gertrude</u>: (invalid from childhood, not married), (died Jan, 1970)

<u>Mary</u>: m. Abraham Edieger (Mary and Henry), (died 1969)

<u>Katherine</u>: m. Henry Rahn (Mary, Peter and Jacob), (died in far eastern Soviet Union in 1942)

<u>Abraham</u>: m. Margaret Harder (Zelma), (last seen 1937-38, taken away by local police or NKVD)

<u>Suzanne</u>: m. Gena (George) Stelzig (Arthur), (born in Konteniusfeld, March 18, 1909; died in Oakland, California, June 2, 1978)

<u>Sara</u>: m. David Hiebert (Nelda), (died in Hanover, West Germany in mid-December 1989 at age 78.)

The Stelzigs:

<u>Father-in-law</u>: Theodore Antonovich (died in Leningrad in 1936)

<u>Mother-in-law</u>: Olga Adamovna (died in Leningrad in 1940)

<u>Children</u>:

<u>Eleanor</u>: (not married, last seen by Suzanne in June, 1941)

<u>Arthur Reinholdt</u>: (not married, last seen 1936, taken away by local police or NKVD)

<u>George (Gena) Theodore</u>: m. Suzanne Penner (last seen in Leningrad when Suzanne left Leningrad in June 1941)

<u>Children</u> - <u>Arthur</u>: m. Evelyn Leggett

100

Grandmother Gertrude (Koop) Penner

Grandmother Penner was very neat and clean, and she was strong and worked very hard. However, she was very jealous of my mother Marie, because she loved her only son (Peter) so much. She sewed and knitted by hand all of my father's clothes. Because of her jealousy, she was a source of conflict in the family. She liked Isaac and Peter, because he was named after her husband, and Gertrude who was named after her, but she was not so loving to the rest of us. Abraham, Suzanne, Sara, Elizabeth, Maria and Katherine, we all had names from my mother's side. But after my mother died in 1928 Grandmother was much different to us, because she sort of took over as mother of the family. She died at about 77 in 1932 or 33 while I was in Makeyevka.

Peter Penner (my father)

My father was spoiled as the only son and he listened more to grandmother than to his wife. He was good-natured (not mean or strict with us), honest and smart. He never would cheat a Russian worker - would always give more to his workers than he promised. He had a cataract on his left eye, so only had one good eye. He was a hard worker and a good farmer, but he really would have liked to be in business, as he was very good with numbers. Every year when the village would go over their accounts (school, roads, sidewalks, etc.), papa would check them to make sure they were in order. He was Burgermeister (mayor) for two years around 1920. He died at 73 on our trek out of Russia in late fall of 1943, and we buried him in a cherry orchard in the small Russian village of Arbousenka not far from the Polish border.

Marie (Franzen) Penner (my mother)

She was from the village of Rudnerweide, about 6 or 7 kilometers east of Konteniusfeld. She had at least two brothers and three sisters, but I only met Uncle Franzen from Grossweide about 5 km east of us. She and papa were married before 1895 (I don't know the year). My parent's first child, named Gertrude, died as a baby, and my oldest brother Isaac was 10 years older than I. It was difficult for my mother because of the conflict in the family caused by grandmother Penner. The children were Gertrude (who died as a baby), Isaac (1896), Peter (1898), Elizabeth (1900), Gertrude (1902), Mary (1903), Katherine (1905), Abraham (1907), Suzanne (1909) and finally Sara (1911). Mother was a quiet, peaceful, hardworking woman who loved and admired her children. She praised grandfather, who died before Abe was born, because he was so helpful with the children. She was brown eyed, had black hair, was slim and was probably very good looking when she was younger. She died of dropsy in 1928 when she was 58.

Isaac Penner (my brother)

Isaac was very smart in school and very inventive. He married Maria Wiens from Konteniusfeld in 1922 and they had four children: Hans, Maria (Mika), Peter and Walter. For the first few years they lived in a small brick house on our farm.

Isaac was always thinking about some new mechanical contraption. During one of the worst times for us he got a job in the mill working on machinery. While there he got 40 pounds of flour, which lasted us for a month. He also shared the bread mother made with the neighbors, older people who were near starvation. During that time we also traded the engine that drove the threshing machine for 2 or 3 sacks of grain (wheat or rye). Later, in about 1925, Isaac felt we needed an engine and he and Dad each went into the village to try to trade some grain for an engine. Isaac was not successful, but Dad got an even larger

102

engine than he had before and still had some grain left over. So Isaac built a frame on wheels for the engine and started threshing for other people who didn't have machines. He would get either the tenth or the fifteenth sack of grain as payment, but this was partly used to pay for oil and gas. He did this until the winter. And then he thought, why should it sit idle, and so he got two huge millstones and built a mill. Abe and Peter ground grain day and night during the winter. This is what really got us through that hard time.

Then Isaac got the idea of getting running water from a good well near Sparrau, a nearby village. He planned to put in the pipes both to Sparrau and to Konteniusfeld to bring fresh water to each house (about 60 houses) in Konteniusfeld. He also had the idea to put in electricity, but about this time (1929 or '30) they formed the collectives and took the threshing machine and engine, so Isaac went to work in Makeyevka, a coal town. First he worked for the Russians as a mechanic, but later for a German firm (Krupps Company) where he worked as an interpreter and as a translator in the library. His family went to Makeyevka about 1932. I last saw Isaac in 1934 when I left for Leningrad. Probably because of jealousy over his good job, the NKVD brought him in for questioning four times in late 1937 and early 1938, and after the last time in February 1938 he was never heard from again.

His family returned to Konteniusfeld. Hans was taken away in 1941 with other men between16 and 65, and Mika died of tuberculosis about 1939. Peter and Walter were on the trek with us out of Russia and in Poland the Germans put then in the army. They were only in the army a few months, when the war was over, and were captured by the Americans in the west. When they were freed, Peter and Walter got together through Mary (Peter and Suzanne Penner's daughter) in West Germany. They came to Schierlin near Niederleierndorf where Margaret and I were staying with the Forsters.

Peter Penner (my brother)

Peter was a happy, hard working farmer who loved animals. He married Suzanne Kliewer from Konteniusfeld. Peter and Suzanne lived on their place near the west end of the village. They had seven children (Suzanne, Mary, Peter, Gertrude, Elizabeth, Hilda and Henry). I last saw Peter in 1934 when I went to Leningrad. Peter was taken away in late 1937 or early 1938 before his last son Henry was born. This would have been about the same time Isaac was taken away. Suzanne stayed on the collective and brought up the seven children. She and all seven children were on the trek with us out of Russia and into Poland. After the war some Mennonites from Canada came to Poland looking for homeless Mennonite people and found her in a camp where she was to be transported back to Russia. They were able to bring Suzanne and her children to Canada.

Elizabeth Penner (my sister)

She married Henry Kasper in 1923 and they had four children: Henry, Mary, Elizabeth (Lisa) and Maria, but Mary died at 2 years of age. Elizabeth was an amazing person - never gave up hope, gave a lot of inspiration to everyone, loved animals, was a good housekeeper and a hard worker - worked like a man. Henry Kasper (her husband) was taken away in 1941. Elizabeth and her children (Henry, Lisa and Maria) were on the trek with us. She drove the wagon that carried her family, our father and Arthur and me. Henry Jr. was taken into the German army in Poland, and the last we heard of him he had been wounded in the head by shrapnel, but the doctor said he would not lose his eyesight. The last I heard from Elizabeth was that she and the two girls were in East Germany, but later they were sent back to the Soviet Union, to the city of New Siberia.

Gertrude Penner (my sister)

Gertrude was about 5 years old when she accidentally had one leg cut off in a wheat cutter. She and Elizabeth were picking cornflowers in the tall wheat and father did not see her until it was too late. She had a wooden leg and helped mostly in the house, but she was a cheerful person and very neat. She did not marry. She was on the wagon train with Mary and was in eastern Germany until she was sent back to New Siberia in the Soviet Union with Mary and her children about 1946. She died in January 1970.

Mary Penner (my sister)

She married Abraham Edieger (from Rudnerweide) and they had two children: Marichen (Maria) and Abraham (Heinz). She was a chatterbox, cheerful, a good housekeeper and mother and was a devoted Christian. The Ediegers moved to Amur Kraj in 1929 (on the Chinese border) but came back about 1931. Abraham was taken away in 1941. Mary and her two children, as well as Gertrude and Walter, who drove, were on a wagon pulled by oxen. Mary, her children and Gertrude were sent back to the Soviet Union shortly after the war. Mary died in 1969.

Katherine Penner (my sister)

She married Henry Krahn (from Rudnerweide) and they had three children: Mary, Peter and Jacob. She was a quiet person, hard working and very capable. Her family moved to Amur Kraj, near the China border in 1929, came back in 1931 and returned to Amur Kraj in 1936. Henry was imprisoned about 1937. Katherine and her children were put on a train with several other women and their children. The women were forced to leave the train at an intermediate stop and the children were taken further on to a Communist youth camp. Mary (about 10 years old) remembered where Katherine had been left off and went back and found her in a hospital. She was ill and she

105

starved to death in the hospital in 1942. Afterward, Mary went back to take care of her brothers, as her mother had asked. When Henry was released from prison, he was reunited with the children. Mary married at a very young age and Peter and Jacob both became engineers. Henry remarried later.

Abraham (Abe) Penner (my brother)

He was quiet, worked hard, loved animals and was a good miller. He married Margaret Harder (from Sparrau) and they had two children: Zelma and a son who died at two years of age. His family lived in a house next to my family's house. I last saw Abe in 1934 when I left for Leningrad. He was last seen when he was taken away in 1937 or 1938. Margaret and Zelma were on the trek with us. They were lucky because they ended up in Niederleierndorf, Byeren (Bavaria) in the American zone. Arthur and I stayed with them at the Forsters after we escaped to the west. They came to Canada through Mr. David Durksen's efforts and settled in Ontario.

Suzanne Penner (Me)

She was more of a 'boy' than a girl. There was not a tree on the farm that she didn't climb and tear her dress. She married George (Gena) Stelzig in Leningrad in 1936 and they had one son, Arthur. She and Arthur were separated from Gena in 1941, when he stayed in Leningrad while they left for the Ukraine, just two days before Germany declared war on the Soviet Union. She and her family, while in Konteniusfeld, were overrun by the Germans in October 1941. In late 1943 they made the long trek in a wagon train to Poland, and then later into Poland and eastern Germany by train. When the war ended in May 1945 she and Arthur found themselves in the Russian Zone near Berlin. She and Arthur escaped to West Germany in 1946. In 1948 they immigrated to Canada with the help of the Durksens, and settled in Pincher Creek, Alberta. In 1957, after marrying Clark Vliet, they moved to Berkeley, California in 1957. Suzanne died in Oakland California on June 2, 1978 and is buried in the Mountain View Cemetery in Oakland.

Sara Penner (my sister)

She married David Hebert (from Orloff) and they had one child, Nelda. Sara was quick and hot-tempered, and she was forthright and very strong willed. David was taken away in 1941. Sara and Nelda were with Margaret and Zelma on the trek to Poland. She got as far as eastern Germany, but shortly after the end of the war the Russians sent her back to Russia (city of New Siberia). David eventually came back and they were reunited through her sister-in-law. But he was ill (had a tumor) and only lived for two more years. Sara and Nelda's family (husband and two girls) applied for and were able to go to East Germany in January 1972. In 1977 Sara was able to come to West Germany. She died in mid-December 1989 in Hanover at age 78.

Other Family Members.

Maria (Wiens) Penner, Isaac's wife. Maria was from Konteniusfeld and she and Isaac married in 1922. They had four children: Hans, Maria (Mika), Peter and Walter. Mika died of tuberculosis in 1939 and Hans was taken away along with several other Mennonite men in 1941. Maria was one of the family members on the trek west in 1943 with Suzanne, and Maria's two sons Peter and Walter accompanied her. Maria was near Berlin when the war ended, and later in 1945 the Russians sent her to Siberia. She spent 20 years there before being able to come to West Germany in 1965. This was after Peter had a chance to talk to Nikita Khrushchev's son-in-law Alexander Adjubej (publisher of a large Moscow Government newspaper) during Adjubej's visit to West Germany in 1965. In 1966 Maria traveled to Canada to see her other son Walter. It was a great reunion but, only 2 weeks after arriving in Canada, Maria had a heart attack and passed away.

Peter Penner (Isaac and Maria's son). Peter was on the trek with his mother Maria and brother Walter. He says he remembers nailing the roof on the wagon they used on the trek west. While in Poland, Peter (and his brother Walter) were conscripted into the German army and served on the western front for a short period before the war was over. He was captured by the American army and served a short time in prison. After his release he settled in Heilbronn, West Germany and had a 40-year career with RWE, a large electric company. In 1986 he retired at age 60 and immigrated to Canada where he settled in Apsley, Ontario, and later in the nearby village of L'Amable, Ontario. Peter passed away in September 2012.

Walter Penner (Isaac and Maria's son). Walter was on the trek with his mother and brother Peter. In Poland he was conscripted into the German army and served for a short time on the western front before he was captured by the American army. After being released from prison he lived for a short time in West Germany, before immigrating to Paraguay where he had a farm. After several years in Paraguay, he and his family moved back to Germany for three years. He immigrated to Canada, and settled in Kitchener, Ontario. Walter passed away in 1987.

18. A Brief History of Mennonite Presence in Russia*

Starting with Peter (the Great), a number of western Europeans were brought into the Russia governmental service to accelerate "westernization" of the country. While Peter emphasized educated administrators and technocrats, Catherine who followed him wanted "pioneering" immigrants who could develop the agricultural resources of Russia. Her second Manifesto of July 22, 1763 included the following guarantees: (1) complete freedom of religious conscience, (2) 'perpetual' exemption from obligatory military service, (3) exemption from taxation for a specified period of time, and (4) communal autonomy in respect to administrative and policing matters. In 1800 Russia's Paul 1 reinforced Catherine's policy, when he enacted a "Privilegium" (set of official privileges) for Mennonites, granting them exemption from military service "for all time". Germany was the ideal recruiting ground. These concessions appealed particularly to those who lived in Prussia and had strong religious feelings, such as the Mennonites. In West Prussia, King Frederick William III was making it difficult for Mennonites to acquire land, because of their refusal to serve in the military. Refuge in Russia was seen as an attractive opportunity. Under Catherine and her successors many such settlers were enticed to immigrate to Russia.

Within a relatively short three-year span after Catherine's Manifesto, some 8,000 German families comprising 27,000 persons settled in the Volga region of Russia. Beginning in 1789, a mass migration of Mennonites from West Prussia took place, and many settled in south Russia. The first of these Mennonite

---

* Taken primarily from Ref. 3 - Molotschna Mennonite Settlement (Zaporizhia Oblast, Ukraine), an article from the Internet.

immigrants were 228 families that settled in the Chortitza and Molotschna colonies. About 60 Mennonite communities were established in southern Russia (the Ukraine), with typically 20 to 40 farms per community. The village of Konteniusfeld was founded in the Molotschna settlement in 1832 (another source says 1821) and named for Samuel Kontenius. It had 25 full-farms and 10 half-farms, and comprised about 8618 acres (another source says 6356 acres). It was located in the eastern portion of the Molotschna settlement about 75 km northwest of Berdjansk, which is near the Azov Sea. The Molotschna area was an enclave of villages which was essentially independent of Russia, as the villages operated their own schools and local governments, and the people spoke German, with only a few able to speak Russian. In the end this isolation went against these communities.

The number of Mennonites in south Russia in the 1870's is estimated at 45,000 and by 1914 about 100,000. Over the century leading up to the 1870's, Russian resentment gradually developed over the favorable concessions held by the Mennonite and other German communities and because of the relative prosperity they had achieved. One of these issues was whether the exemptions were "perpetual" or to last for "one century". One of the Russian words used in the agreements was ambiguous. 'Vjek' can mean 'century', but it can also mean 'eternity', and it was declared that the term of privileges had come to an end, since a century had passed. As a result of this, almost half of the Mennonites who had been in the Ukraine during the 1870's immigrated to the United States and Canada over the next few years. In spite of this exodus, the Mennonite population in the Ukraine continued to increase until 1914. During this time a number of daughter Mennonite communities were established in the Crimea, the Caucasus, the Volga and Ufa/Orenburg regions closer to the Ural Mountains, as well as in Siberia.

In 1915, the Russian journalist A. Rennikov, in his Soloto Reina (Gold of the Rhine) press campaign against the Russo-

Germans, demanded their liquidation. He argued that even if Russia defeated Germany in a war and drove the German soldiers out of Russia, there would still be two million Germans in Russia, who would "continue to ruin the Russian peasantry". When the Soviet Union was established following the Revolution and Civil War, it annulled all Tsarist decrees, thus saving Mennonites and other Germans from ruin for a few years. During 1924-29 a large number of Mennonites left Russia for Canada, but this was the last exodus, as the Soviet Union thereafter closed its borders. With the coming of 'collectivization' and the taking away of many of their able-bodied men, the Mennonite's faith and trust in their host-land were shattered. See Molotschna Colony map below.

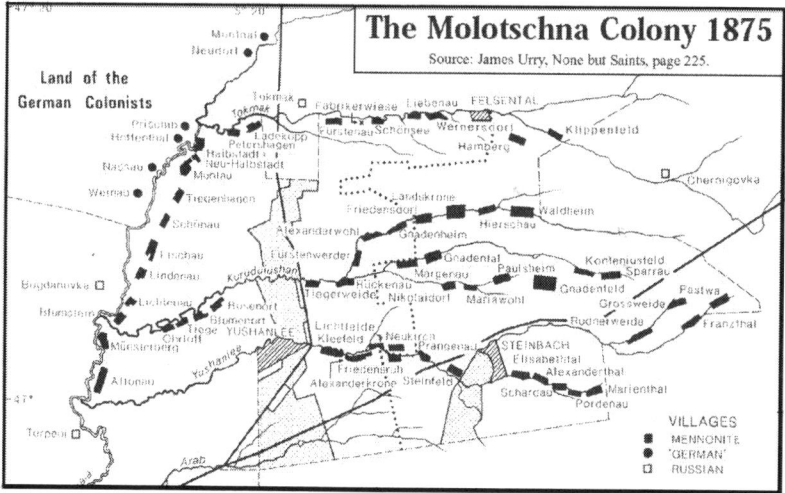

The Molotschna Colony 1875
Source: James Urry, None but Saints, page 225.

Land of the German Colonists

VILLAGES
- MENNONITE
- 'GERMAN'
- RUSSIAN

The Molotschna Colony as of 1875. Konteniusfeld and Sparrau are located near the middle-right. The part-year stream adjacent to them is the Kutudujuschan, and the larger stream it empties into is the Molotschna River, for which the colony was named. Note that along the west side of the Molotschna there are several German-Lutheran communities and there were a few Russian villages on the periphery of the settlement. Map obtained from Ref. 5 & 6. Used with permission.

19. Afterword

In the spring of 1972, the first year that we lived in Austin, our family went skiing to Colorado. Our son was a baby and our girls just toddlers, so we asked Suzanne, who was living in Berkeley, to meet us in Colorado and then come to Austin for a visit. So she flew to Denver and took care of the kids during the day. It was a lot of fun for all of us, and it was also a good opportunity for our children to get to know Suzanne better.

After the ski trip we drove back to Austin where Suzanne stayed for about two weeks. One of my favorite things about Suzanne, beyond her great dinners, was hearing about her experiences in the Soviet Union and escaping to the West. During her visit that spring, she related several of these experiences. About three or four days before she was to return to Berkeley, the thought came to me that I should tape that part of her life. So I got a pad of paper and we started making a chronological outline of her life, starting from her first recollections as a child all the way through Arthur getting married. The first night about all we did was make outlines, three or four times, each one becoming more and more detailed. The next night we started taping on my old Sony recorder. As I recall, we taped for several hours on each of two nights, filling up several tapes, which I still have. I don't recall whether I intended to write up the material or not. I any case, Suzanne returned to California.

Shortly thereafter I arranged to have the recorded material typed. However typing from the tapes proved to be difficult as they were regular cassettes, not stenographic. So I borrowed a stenographic tape recorder and transcribed the material onto those cassettes, simply by playing through the speaker of one into the microphone of the other ... pretty low-tech! This facilitated the typing of the material, but the sound quality was poor and as a result there were many holes in the manuscript. Over several months I went through the typed material, and using the original tapes filled in as best I could. I sent a copy of the rough material to Suzanne, asking her to go over it and fill in, correct, add to, or whatever so as to make it as complete as possible. Well, she never did. It is interesting that Suzanne never dwelt on the difficult times in her life and probably just didn't find editing the material very worthwhile. She had more important things to do with her life ... participating in the First Presbyterian Church women's sewing group, sending goods to relatives in the Soviet Union, and of course taking care of "her men".

Suzanne and author working on her story in Austin, Texas in Spring 1972. Taken by Donna.

In conversations with my brother Les late in 1977, he indicated that having to take care of Dad (he was becoming senile) was taking a toll on Suzanne. To give Suzanne a break, he had taken Dad to Grants Pass to be with my sister Shirley's family. We all thought it would be a good change of scene if Suzanne were to come to Austin for a while. Although she was very weak when she arrived, after being with us for a short period, without the concern and demands of Dad, she improved remarkably. She was with us for about three weeks over Christmas of 1977. During the latter part of this stay with us, I got her to spend several hours going over the written material. We only got through about half of it, but did fill in a lot and add to it greatly. If one looks at the material, it is apparent that there is more detail in the first half than in the last. I wish we could have edited it all, as I'm sure there are lots of other interesting stories she had to tell. In putting this material together, it is probably unfortunate that I had to do significant editing of the material from the tapes to make it more readable, because in so doing, a lot of Suzanne's colorful language and personality does not come through. We'll just have to remember her as she was.

In the spring of 1978 it became apparent that Suzanne was very ill. Arthur and I flew to Berkeley and all three boys, Arthur, Les and I were there, when Suzanne passed away in Oakland on June 2, 1978. The funeral was held at First Presbyterian Church in Berkeley. One of the real regrets I've had is that I didn't talk to the minister who officiated, to have him give a more personal sermon. Suzanne likely had a more interesting and eventful life than anyone in that church, but his sermon was about as impersonal as it could have been! Suzanne was buried at the Mountain View Cemetery in Oakland, California, on a hillside that looks out across the Bay toward San Francisco.

It is an understatement to say that, "To those of us who knew her, Suzanne was truly an unforgettable person."

****

Trip to the Ukraine – July 2012

For several years I have yearned to visit Suzanne's childhood village of Konteniusfeld, and in the summer of 2012 the opportunity arose. My wife Donna and I were invited to Turkey to participate in a student summer-abroad program and we decided to visit the Ukraine after our time in Turkey. Through Dr. James Urry I was put in contact with Olga Shmakina, who arranged a trip for us through the Intourist Travel Agency in Zaporizhia. On July 9 we flew into Dnipropetrovs'k from Istanbul and were driven about 60 km south to Zaporizhia, where we stayed for three nights. The next day Olga was our guide for a full day trip to the Molotschna Mennonite settlement. After seeing a number of interesting buildings in several villages, including Halbstadt and Gnadenfeld, we arrived in Konteniusfeld. The names of all (or most) of the Mennonite villages, which were German, have been changed ... the villages of Konteniusfeld and Sparrau have grown together since the 1940's and are now named Dovhe. The town of Gnadenfeld is now Bohdanivka.

Olga had a map showing the locations of the various Mennonite families in the village before the war. On arriving in the village we were fortunate to ask directions from Gennadiy Peznikov, who is a schoolteacher and 'somewhat the local historian'. Between the map and Mr. Peznikov we were able to identify the location of the old Penner place on the south side of the street and the second lot to the west of the lane leading to the cemetery. Mr. Peznikov said he grew up in Sparrau (after the war) and as a boy remembered the house just to the east of the Penners, which had been an "ice-house". On asking Mr. Peznikov if we could visit the senior Penner place, he told us the elderly woman living there would not likely welcome us, but he would check with the family next door. He inquired of the young family living there, Andrei Didenko and his wife, and they were more that gracious. We did not see the inside of their house, but they showed us their water well (which was apparently one of the better wells in town), and their chicken house in the back. That day Mrs. Didenko was doing the wash by hand in a tub in the back yard and had the washing up to dry. The house was not the original Mennonite house that had belonged to Isaac Penner, but one that had been rebuilt presumably on the same foundation sometime since the war. The senior Penner house next door (Suzanne's old home) had also been rebuilt. There was only one original Mennonite house still standing in the village* ... many of them were destroyed during the German retreat, or so badly damaged they had since been torn down and rebuilt. While with the Didenkos, Mr. Peznikov asked if I would like a memento of our visit and I was given two clay roof tiles. The tiles had been manufactured by the Abram Kasper Brick Company, and cast into the tiles are the words: A. Kasper and Konteniusfeld (in Russian). These tiles most likely came from the old Isaac Penner house, but possibly could have come from the 'senior' Penner house next door. The tiles on the current Didenko house appear to be similar, and the old tiles were likely used for the roof in the current house. Both tiles were broken during their shipment back on the plane, but have been bonded back together and one was sent to Arthur. Suzanne's sister Elizabeth was married to Henry Kasper.

The pictures that follow show several views of Konteniusfeld: the road sign directing us to Dovhe (Konteniusfeld-Sparrau), the poplar-lined road leading to Dovhe, the old 'senior' Penner place (Donna by the front gate) and several pictures of the old Isaac Penner place: view from the entrance, the well on the property, Mrs. Didenko washing clothes, several people conversing (current house and Kasper roof tiles in the background), and Donna and me with the

----

* See p. 122.

116

Didenkos. Finally, photos of the top and bottom of one of the tiles are shown with the 'A. Kasper' and 'Konteniusfeld' impressions in Russian evident.

Road sign directing us to Dohve (Konteniusfeld/Sparrau)

Poplar lined road leading to Konteniusfeld (Dohve)

Donna by the entrance to the old senior Penner place.

Mr. Peznikov and Olga near front of the Didenko home
(the previous Isaac Penner place).

Several people chatting behind the Didenko home.
Note the "Kasper" tiles on the roof.

Water well on the Didenko place.

Mrs. Didenko doing the family wash.

Donna and author with Andrei Didenko and his wife
and her father on the far left.

Views of the underside (left enlarged) and top (right) of one of the roof tiles that were given to me. Note the words 'A. Kasper' and 'Konteniusfeld' (in Russian) in the left view. The tiles were in almost perfect condition when given to me in Konteniusfeld, but were broken on two corners during the plane trip back. One was given to Art Stelzig.

Before leaving the village, our guide took us by the sole surviving complete house in Konteniusfeld from the Mennonite period (see following page). Other houses in the village may retain portions of original structures, but this presumably is the only complete house. It is of masonry (brick) construction, as were essentially all the houses, and painted white with windows in blue trim ... very attractive. It is across the street and a few houses east of the old Penner places.

121

Only surviving (complete) house in Konteniusfeld from the Mennonite period and its picturesque window. This house is across the street from the old Penner places, and a few houses to the east.

The map of the village of Konteniusfeld below shows the locations of the various Mennonite families as of the 1930's. The map is from: Halmut T. Huebert, Molotschna Historical Atlas (Springfield Publishers, Winnipeg, 2003) p. 52, and was prepared by Maria Kasper. On the south side of the main street beginning with the lots to the west of the lane leading to the cemetery, the lots read: Ice House; Abraham Penner and Peter Penner and Kindergarten; Isaak Penner; Jacob Thissen; Heinrich Siebert, etc. Isaak was the eldest son and lived on the lot next to the senior Penner place. Abraham was the youngest son and his house was on the senior Penner lot. The middle son (Peter) had a place in the northwest part of the village on the north side of the street (fourth lot from the west end of the village). The Abram Kasper

Map of the village of Konteniusfeld in the 1930's with Mennonite property owners indicated. Prepared by Maria Kasper. Ref. 12.

123

Bick Factory was located at the west end of the village on the north side of the main street. Suzanne's sister Elizabeth was married to Henry Kasper. The footnote indicates the Abram Kasper Brick Factory and the Johann Toews Windmill were destroyed during collectivization.

Before leaving Konteniusfeld to return to Zaporizhia, we visited the railroad station at Stulnjevo about 18 km north. The Stulnjevo station is where thousands of Mennonites had been assembled for shipment east in 1941, but their leaving was foiled by the train track being sabotaged. This is also the station from which Suzanne left for Leningrad in 1934 and returned with Arthur in June 1941.

The old railway station at Stulnjevo, which appeared to be in good condition, even though a nearby newer station had been built during the Communist era. This station is where some 7000 Mennonites were assembled for shipment east in the Fall of 1941, but this did not take place. This is also the station from which Suzanne departed for Leningrad in 1934 and returned to with Arthur in June 1941.

Some Reflections on the Economic Conditions of the Current Villagers and Ukraine in general.

I initially had mixed feeling about visiting Konteniusfeld, in that I would be seeing houses/places that had once been owned and lived in by Suzanne's people, but were now occupied by descendants of "squatters". But on further consideration, I realized that to a large extent her family's ultimate loss was largely a result of the war and their forced evacuation by the German army, even though their life and property ownership had been upturned under Communism. The people now occupying the former Mennonite houses presumably had just "assumed" ownership of vacated houses in the turmoil of the German retreat of 1943. In hindsight, and if I had been able to speak Ukrainian or Russian, it would be interesting to have heard the stories of those who settled into the Mennonite villages immediately after the German retreat. For example, how did the occupancy take place and how chaotic was it?

We saw only the southern part of the Ukraine, not Kiev or Odessa, but the poverty of the villages is particularly obvious. The poor economy of Ukraine is obvious, even in some of the urban areas. At the Dnipropetrovs'k airport, where we arrived and departed, the security was decades behind. In Zaporizhia many of the buildings along Lenin Avenue appeared to be unoccupied and the emissions from factories on the outskirts of town as seen from our hotel window were ominously "grey and orange". Even though Ukraine split from the Soviet Union in 1991 (over two decades ago), the statue of Lenin at the end of 'Lenin Avenue' was still there and the avenue name had not been changed, apparently because of the undue economic cost to the city and local businesses. The main roads were reasonably good, but in the villages (in places) they were horrid! In a couple of small villages a few miles to the west of Konteniusfeld the broken up asphalt pavement, now "islands' of asphalt separated by bare dirt, was so bad that the driver had to weave back and forth across the road and frequently come to a near stop! A dirt road would have been much superior, except I suppose during the "muddy" season!

In Konteniusfeld, as well as other villages, many houses were destroyed or badly damaged during the German invasion and later retreat. In the course of the 70 years since the War, it is assumed that many of the houses were occupied for a while, but in the course of time most were torn down and rebuilt. In Konteniusfeld only one original Mennonite house exists*, of the approximately 100 houses there at the time of the War. On both the former senior Penner and Isaac Penner properties the houses have been rebuilt, presumably on the original foundations and largely with materials reclaimed from the original houses. It was after we returned from the trip that I noticed the roof tiles on the Didenko house (note photo of the group with the house in the background) appeared to be the same as the tiles I was given. Wood is not readily available in the Molotschna area, so a lot of the materials for new or rebuilt structures (brick, tile and wood) were likely reclaimed from the original houses.

When we arrived at the Didenko home, Mrs. Didenko was doing "the wash" in a tub on the ground outside by the well, with much clothing on the line to dry. The scene was a bit like one would envision from "The Grapes of Wrath". While the family's situation was not bright, it appeared to us that they were not unhappy ... still we both had empathy for them.

The reason for the plight of Ukraine is interesting. During the pre-collective era of the Mennonites, each villager owned a small property "in the village", and a larger acreage (20 to 40 hectares) in the proximity. Each property in the village included the area for the house as well as for a good-sized garden in the back. Suzanne spoke lovingly about their gardens and orchards.

----

* See p. 122.

126

The larger acreages where they grew their main crops ... wheat, barely, etc., were on the outskirts of the village. During the Mennonite period, when the area was collectivized, the 'larger' acreages became part of the collective, as I presume did the home sites. Following the war the villagers continued the collective system until Ukraine became independent in 1991. When the Ukraine broke away from the Soviet Union the collective system was abandoned, so what was to be done with the large "communal" acreages? What the new government did was sell off the agricultural acreage to those who had the capital, and this resulted in very large farms. Villagers under the collective system had little capital of their own and all they could retain were their homes and small garden areas. The result is that the current villagers must rely upon their small lots for a livelihood and also undoubtedly seek secondary employment with the now large landholders. And the villagers appear to be living at a rather low economic level.

As we drove through rural Ukraine we remarked at the vast, unending fields of sunflowers. Our guide related that sunflowers were now the "cash crop" and many (most) of the farms have begun growing sunflowers exclusively. And she commented that they have been growing sunflowers to the detriment of the soil, which becomes nutrient poor after several uninterrupted years of growing the same crop. So this is a concern for the future ... does one of the Ukraine's best commodities (agriculture) take a hit because of poor farming practice. The old Mennonite style was certainly much more sustainable and better for people in the villages.

Finally, Ukraine is in a precarious situation with its neighbor Russia. Ukraine is short in energy resources and depends to a significant extent on natural gas from Russia, but Russia has been holding Ukraine hostage in that regard.

While to my knowledge no Mennonites still live in the Molotschna area, we were heartened to see that their influence is still being felt. In Halbstadt (now Molochansk) we visited a former Mennonite school for girls, which had been restored and is being used as a resource primarily for senior citizens. While we were there (and served lunch), several seniors were involved in a craft or discussion group in one of the rooms. The 'center' was restored about ten years ago by "Friends of the Mennonite Center of Ukraine", a Canadian group, and the organization continues to support it's work. In Petershagen, a few miles from Halbstadt we visited the restored Petershagen (Mennonite) church and there we met a teenage girl who was doing volunteer work for an upcoming summer youth camp. The church was restored about ten years ago with funds raised by George Schroeder (son of the last minister before it closed) from the United States and Frank Dyck from Canada. I understand that in other villages there are similar building restorations, which have also been funded by Mennonite groups in the U.S. and Canada.

The preceding was written in 2013, prior to the serious early 2014 demonstrations in Kiev and the Russian takeover of the Crimea, and as this goes to press the future of Ukraine is in question.

Gary Vliet, Spring 2014

512-731-6100

gvliet6333@gmail.com

Some Sources

1. Gedenkbuechlein (an account of the 'trek' which includes several pictures of the 'trek', and has the 'trek' picture of Suzanne on its cover), by P.H. Dirks, Virgil, Ontario, June 1951. (in German).

2. Molotschna Historical Atlas, by Helmut Huebert. Published by Springfield Publishers, Winnipeg, Manitoba, Canada. 2003

3. Molotschna Mennonite Settlement (Zaporizhia Oblast, Ukraine), an article from the Internet.
www.gameo.org/encyclopedia/contents/M6521.html

4. KRIM-GR Research Website (on Mennonites). History of the Mennonite Settlers, an article from the Internet.
www.icehouse.net/debbie.html/mennonites.html

5. Background Genealogy – Molotschna Summaries. A history of the Molotschna Settlement, with maps and population data, including James Urry's map of the Molotschna Colony. From Kraus House Info-Research Solutions.
www.krausehouse.ca/krause/Molotschna.html

6. None but Saints, The Transformation of Mennonite Life in Russia 1789-1889, by James Urry. Map of Molotschna Colony appears on page 225. Used with permission.

7. Conrad Grebel University College, www.grebel.uwaterloo.ca/ Picture of Suzanne during the 'Trek', purchased from this source.

8. Global Anabaptist Mennonite Encyclopedia, www.gameo.org/

9. Autobiography of Peter Penner (Suzanne's nephew). A draft of Peter's autobiography (in development as of October 2010).

129

10. Map of the Mennonite families living in Konteniusfeld prior to 1943, prepared by Maria Kasper. From Halmut T. Huebert, Molotschna Historical Atlas (Springfield Publishers, Winnipeg, 2003).

11. Olga Shmakina with the Intourist Travel Agency in Zaporizhia. Olga was our tour guide for the July 10th day trip to the Molotschna Mennonite Settlement. She provided several pieces of information on the settlement and Konteniusfeld, including the map of the village. (see Ref. 10)

12. Article from Wikipedia on Lady Muriel Paget. http://en.wikipedia.org/wiki/Muriel_Paget

Photo of Suzanne during the Trek – Purchased from Ref. 7. Used with permission.

Molotschna Map – from "None but Saints" (p. 225), by James Urry, which appears in Krause House Info-Research Solutions, www.kraushouse.ca/krause/Molotschna.htm Used with permission.

Map of Suzanne's travels – composed by the author on a blank Rand McNally map of Western Europe.

Plan of the Penner house. Composed from Suzanne's description of her family's house in Konteniusfeld.

Various documents, as well as pictures of Suzanne, Gena and Arthur – from Arthur Stelzig and from materials left by Suzanne.

Recent pictures from Konteniusfeld, from the author's trip to the Molotschna area in July 2012.

Map of Konteniusfeld in the 1930's. From Halmut T. Huebert, Molotschna Historical Atlas (Springfield Publishers, Winnipeg, 2003) p. 52, prepared by Maria Kasper.

Acknowledgements and Permissions

First of all, I thank Suzanne for telling me her story and also for relating snippets of her story to many family members who remember them well.

I appreciate Patty Adams' effort in typing Suzanne's story from the original audiotapes. I acknowledge Peter Penner (now deceased) for the story about the Soviets finally allowing his mother to come to the west and also for reviewing some of the details of Suzanne's story. I also thank Arthur for reviewing details of his mother's (and his) story, for providing his input as Suzanne's son, and for a number of the photographs included herein. I acknowledge the several family recollections that were part of an earlier version of this book but, except for Arthur's, have been omitted from the current more 'public' version. I also appreciate Robert Waits (an old friend) for advice on publishing. Finally, I appreciate my wife Donna for several suggestions, for a couple pictures used, and for her forbearance during the writing of Suzanne's story.

I acknowledge Dr. James Urry for several edits offered. I'm much indebted to Olga Shmakina for serving as our guide during our July 2012 trip to the Molotschna area, and for making me aware of the Konteniusfeld village map. We were also fortunate to meet Gennadiy Peznikov in Konteniusfeld who introduced us to the Didenkos ... and we are particularly appreciative of the Andrei Didenko family, who met with us and when leaving gave me two 'Kasper' roof tiles as souvenirs of our visit.

Three items were reproduced from other sources. I acknowledge 'Conrad Grebel University College' for the 'Trek' photo, which was purchased from its library. I acknowledge Springfield Publishers for use of the Konteniusfeld village map published in the 'Molotschna Historical Atlas' by Halmut T. Huebert and Dr. James Urry for his permission to use the 'Molotschna Colony' map published in his 'None but Saints'.

The Author

Gary Vliet was born in Alberta where he spent his growing up years. He graduated from the University of Alberta and continued studies at Stanford, before a career first at Lockheed in Palo Alto and then teaching Mechanical Engineering at the University of Texas at Austin, until he retired in 2006. He and his wife Donna live in Austin, Texas.

He first met Suzanne about 1954 when she was working at the boarding house where his future brother-in-law lived. After Suzanne and his father Clark Vliet were married and moved to Berkeley, he and Donna had many enjoyable weekend dinners there and Suzanne became like a second mother to him and a mother and grandmother to other members of the family. She is missed, but many of us have cherished memories.

The author in a field of sunflowers near Konteniusfeld. Sunflowers are a 'major' agricultural crop throughout the southern Ukraine.

133